SUMMER MATH WORKBOOK

Bridge Building Activities

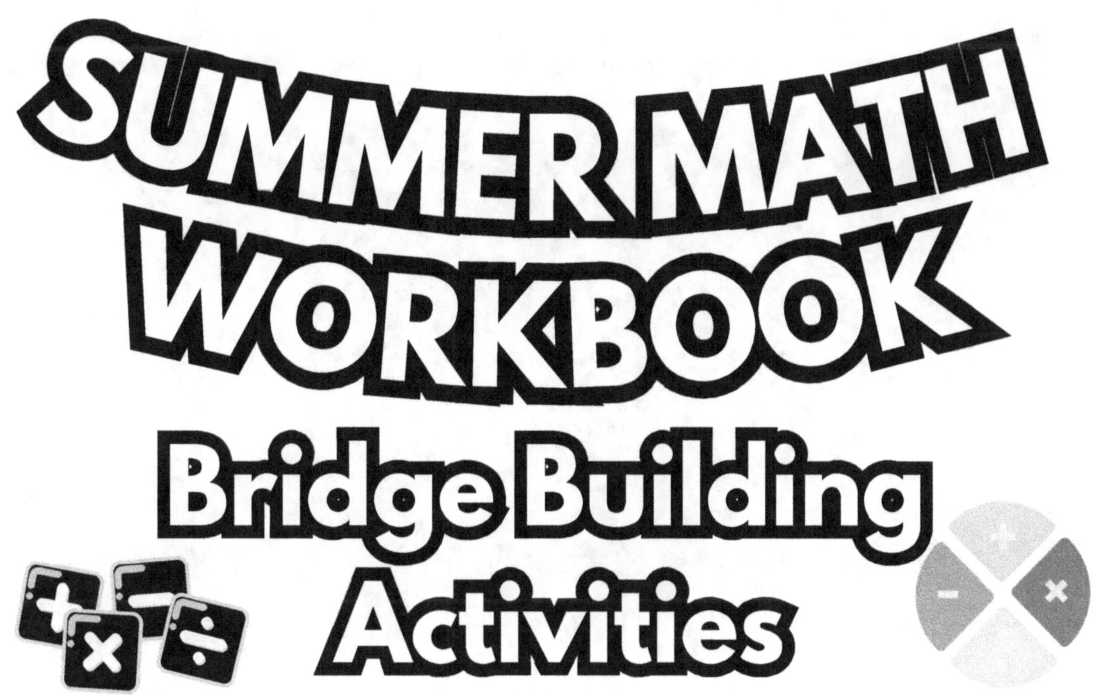

Introduction

As parents and educators, we understand the pivotal role that mathematics plays in shaping a child's academic journey and future success. Yet, the path to mathematical proficiency can often seem daunting, filled with challenges and complexities. That's where the transformative power of Summer Bridge Building Activities books comes into play, illuminating the way forward with clarity, precision, and purpose.

Summer vacation is a time for rest and relaxation, but it also presents the risk of the "summer slide," where students lose some of the academic gains they made during the school year. Summer Bridge Building Activities books are specifically designed to tackle this challenge, ensuring that your child stays academically engaged and prepared for the upcoming school year. These books provide a seamless bridge from one grade to the next, reinforcing essential skills and introducing new concepts that will give your child a head start.

Imagine your child eagerly diving into the pages of a Summer Bridge Building Activities book, greeted by clear, engaging content that demystifies complex mathematical concepts. With each turn of the pages, they embark on a journey of discovery, encountering thoughtfully curated practice questions that reinforce learning and sharpen problem-solving skills. As they unveil the answers to those questions, a sense of accomplishment blossoms within them — a tangible reward for their hard work and dedication.

Summer Bridge Building Activities books transcend traditional educational tools; they are meticulously crafted to build a deep and enduring understanding of mathematics. These books follow a sequential and logical progression, starting from fundamental principles and advancing to sophisticated problem-solving strategies. Each chapter is designed to build on the previous one, ensuring a solid and comprehensive foundation for future learning.

Parents, we yearn for nothing more than to see our children thrive academically and personally. We want to witness the spark of inspiration ignited within them as they overcome academic challenges with confidence and poise. Summer Bridge Building Activities books serve as indispensable partners in this noble endeavor, offering not just practice questions but the keys to unlocking a world of academic and personal opportunities.

Visualize the pride on your child's face as they master a challenging math concept, the joy they experience when their efforts yield results, and the confidence they gain with each success. These pages are designed to make learning math a positive, enriching, and deeply rewarding experience that will benefit them throughout their academic journey and beyond.

For educators, Summer Bridge Building Activities books are invaluable allies in the quest to cultivate mathematical proficiency in the classroom. Accompanied by comprehensive guides and readily available answers, instructors can focus on mentoring and nurturing their students, secure in the knowledge that these books provide a robust framework for effective learning.

Within the pages of Summer Bridge Building Activities books lies not just the promise of academic excellence, but the seeds of a brighter future. By integrating these resources into your child's summer routine, you are bestowing upon them the gifts of confidence, curiosity, and a lifelong love of learning.

Invest in your child's future today with Summer Bridge Building Activities books — because every great journey begins with a single step, and this step can change everything. Keep the momentum of learning alive over the summer, and watch your child soar to new academic heights.

Contents

Grade
1 → 2
SUMMER MATH WORKBOOK
Bridge Building Activities
Number Sense
Addition and Subtraction
Place Value

Grade
2 → 3
SUMMER MATH WORKBOOK
Bridge Building Activities
Number Sense
Addition and Subtraction
Place Value

Grade
3 → 4
SUMMER MATH WORKBOOK
Bridge Building Activities
Number Sense
Addition and Subtraction
Place Value

Grade
4 → 5
SUMMER MATH WORKBOOK
Bridge Building Activities
Multiplication and Division
Place Value and Units
Fractions and Geometry

Grade
5 → 6
SUMMER MATH WORKBOOK
Bridge Building Activities
Multiplication and Division
Factors and Multiples
Fractions and Geometry

Grade
6 → 7
SUMMER MATH WORKBOOK
Bridge Building Activities
Arithmetic
Algebra
Geometry and Statistics

Grade
7 → 8
SUMMER MATH WORKBOOK
Bridge Building Activities
Ratio and Percentage
Algebra and Cartesian Plane
Geometry and Statistics

Grade
8 → 9
SUMMER MATH WORKBOOK
Bridge Building Activities
Ratio and Percentage
Algebra
Geometry and Graphing

Grade
9 → 10
SUMMER MATH WORKBOOK
Bridge Building Activities
Factoring and Distributing
Algebra
Geometry and Graphing

<u>Addition and Subtraction</u>

<u>Addition with Regrouping</u>

When we do addition, we combine numbers. But sometimes, when we're adding numbers, we might need to regroup. Regrouping means we have to move a number from one place to another, usually to the next column, to get the right answer.

For Example: Let's take an example of adding 6533 and 7579 together:

$$\begin{array}{r} 6\ 5\ 3\ 3 \\ +\underline{7\ 5\ 7\ 9} \end{array}$$

First, we start by adding the digits in the ones place: 3 + 9 = 12. We write down the 2 in the ones place and carry over the 1 to the tens place.

$$\begin{array}{r} 1 \\ 6\ 5\ 3\ 3 \\ +\underline{7\ 5\ 7\ 9} \\ 2 \end{array}$$

Now, we add the digits in the tens place, along with the carry-over: 3 + 7 + 1 = 11. We write down the 1 in the tens place and carry over the 1 to the hundreds place.

$$\begin{array}{r} 1\ 1 \\ 6\ 5\ 3\ 3 \\ +\underline{7\ 5\ 7\ 9} \end{array}$$

Now, we add the digits in the hundreds place, along with the carry-over: 5 + 5 + 1 = 11. We write down the 1 in the tens place and carry over the 1 to the hundreds place.

$$
\begin{array}{r}
1\ 1\ 1\ \\
6\ 5\ 3\ 3 \\
+\ 7\ 5\ 7\ 9 \\
\hline
1\ 1\ \ 2
\end{array}
$$

Now, we add the digits in the thousandth place, along with the carry-over: 6 + 7 + 1 = 14.

$$
\begin{array}{r}
1\ 1\ 1\ \\
6\ 5\ 3\ 3 \\
+\ 7\ 5\ 7\ 9 \\
\hline
1\ 4\ 1\ 1\ 2
\end{array}
$$

This process of carrying over helps us accurately add numbers, especially when they're larger.

Subtraction with Regrouping

Subtraction is a key math operation where we find the difference between two numbers. Sometimes, when we subtract, we might need to regroup, which means borrowing from the next column.

Let's take an example of subtracting 8436 from 6563:

First, we start by subtracting the digits in the ones place: 3 - 6.

Since 3 is less than 6, we need to regroup. We borrow 1 from the tens place, making it 5 tens instead of 6, and add it to the ones place.

So, 3 becomes 13, and then we subtract 6.

$$8\ 5\ 6\ \mathbf{13}$$
$$\underline{-6\ 4\ 3\ 6}$$
$$7$$

Now, we subtract the tens place digits: 5 - 3 = 2

$$\mathbf{5}$$
$$8\ 5\ \cancel{6}\ 13$$
$$\underline{-6\ 4\ 3\ 6}$$
$$2\ 7$$

Now, we subtract the hundreds place digits: 5 - 4 = 1

$$\mathbf{5}$$
$$8\ 5\ \cancel{6}\ 13$$
$$\underline{-6\ 4\ 3\ 6}$$
$$1\ 2\ 7$$

Now, we subtract the hundreds place digits: 8 - 6 = 2

$$\mathbf{5}$$
$$8\ 5\ \cancel{6}\ 13$$
$$\underline{-6\ 4\ 3\ 6}$$
$$2\ 1\ 2\ 7$$

This process of regrouping or borrowing helps us accurately subtract numbers, especially when the top digit is smaller than the bottom one.

Multiplication and Division

Multiplication

Multiplication is an easy way of adding numbers together quickly. Instead of adding the same number repeatedly, we use multiplication to find the total much faster.

For instance, rather than adding 2 + 2 + 2 + 2 + 2, we can multiply 2 by 5 to get the same result: 2 x 5 = 10.

Here, the first number (2) is called the multiplicand, second number (5) is the multiplier. The answer we get, in this case, 10, is called the product.

Let's think of multiplication as repeated addition.

Take 2 x 5, for example. It means adding 2 together five times, which we can illustrate as: 2 + 2 + 2 + 2 + 2 = 10

Multiplication can also be visualized as groups of objects. Imagine we have 2 groups, each containing 5 oranges.

To find the total number of oranges, we multiply the number of groups (2) by the number of oranges in each group (5):

2 groups of 5 oranges = 10 oranges

Expressed as multiplication: 2 x 5 = 10

In summary, multiplication offers various ways to approach it: through repeated addition or by envisioning groups of objects. It's a powerful tool that makes solving math problems much quicker and more efficient!

We can also use the following table to quickly remember multiplication facts. The intersection of two points shows the product of two numbers.

For instance, the product of 5 x 6 = 30, or 6 x 5 = 30.

Division

Division is like the opposite of multiplication. It's all about sharing or distributing items equally among a certain number of groups or people.

When we divide one number by another, we're essentially splitting a number into equal parts. We're figuring out how many groups of a certain size can be made from that number.

For instance, let's divide 20 by 4.

When we divide 20 by 4, we're essentially asking, "How many groups of size 4 can we make from 20?"

Now, there are several parts or terms involved in the division process:

- **Dividend:** This is the number being divided, which in this case, is 20.

- **Divisor:** This is the number we're dividing by, which is 4.

- **Quotient:** This is the answer we get after dividing. It tells us how many groups of divisors can be made from the dividend. In this case, the answer is 5.

So, when we divide 20 by 4, we found out that 5 groups of 4 can be made from 20.

Decimals

Adding Decimals

Adding decimals is like adding whole numbers, but we must align the decimal points carefully. For instance, when adding 49.88 and 45.78:

Step 1: Align the decimal points.

49.88

+ 45.78

Step 2: Start adding from the rightmost digit (the ones place) and move to the left.

 Add 8 and 8: 8 + 8 = 16. Write down 6 in the ones place and carry over 1 to the tenths place.

49.88

+ 45.78

6

Step 3: Add the tenths place.

Add 1 (carried over from the previous step), 8, and 7: 1 + 8 + 7 = 16. Write down 6 in the tenths place and carry over 1 to the hundredths place.

49.88

+ 45.78

66

Step 4: Continue adding digits to the left until you reach the leftmost digit:

49.88

+ 45.78

9566

Step 5: Finally, write the sum with the decimal point directly below the decimal points in the original numbers.

$$\begin{array}{r} 49.88 \\ +\ \underline{45.78} \\ 95.66 \end{array}$$

Subtracting Decimals

Subtracting decimals follows a process like adding decimals, except instead of adding the numbers, we subtract them.

<u>**Place Value and Expanded Notations**</u>

Place value tells us the value of a digit in a number based on where it's placed.

Consider the number **536.824**. It consists of six digits: 5, 3, 6, 8, 2, and 4.

Digit	Place Value Position	Value Calculation	Value
5	Hundred thousands place	5 × 100,000	500,000
6	Ten thousands place	6 × 10,000	60,000
5	Thousands place	5 × 1,000	5,000
3	Hundreds place	3 × 100	300
4	Tens place	4 × 10	40
7	Ones place	7 × 1	7
2	Tenths place	2 × 0.1	0.2
3	Hundredths place	3 × 0.01	0.03
6	Thousandths place	6 × 0.001	0.006

Each digit occupies a unique position:

- The digit **5** is in the hundred thousands place, signifying five groups of 100,000.

- The digit **6** is in the ten thousands place, indicating six groups of 10,000.

- The digit **5** is in the thousands place, representing five groups of 1,000.

- The digit **3** is in the hundreds place, representing three groups of 100.

- The digit **4** is in the tens place, representing four groups of 10.

- The digit **7** is in the ones place, representing seven single units.

- The digit **2** is in the tenths place, representing two groups of 0.1.

- The digit **3** is in the hundredths place, representing three groups of 0.01.

- The digit **6** is in the thousandths place, representing six groups of 0.001.

To find the total value of the number **565,347.236**, we calculate the value of each digit based on its place:

- The digit **5** in the hundred thousands place equals 500,000.

- The digit **6** in the ten thousands place equals 60,000.

- The digit **5** in the thousands place equals 5,000.

- The digit **3** in the hundreds place equals 300.

- The digit **4** in the tens place equals 40.

- The digit **7** in the ones place equals 7.

- The digit **2** in the tenths place equals 0.2.

- The digit **3** in the hundredths place equals 0.03.

- The digit **6** in the thousandths place equals 0.006.

By summing these values, we determine the overall value of the number:

$$500{,}000 + 60{,}000 + 5{,}000 + 300 + 40 + 7 + 0.2 + 0.03 + 0.006 = 565{,}347.236$$

<u>Fractions</u>

Fractions represent parts of a whole. They consist of a numerator (the number on top) and a denominator (the number on the bottom).

For example: we have an orange, and we divide it into 5 equal slices. Each slice represents $\frac{1}{5}$ of the orange. Now, if we take 3 of those slices, we have taken $\frac{3}{5}$ of the orange.

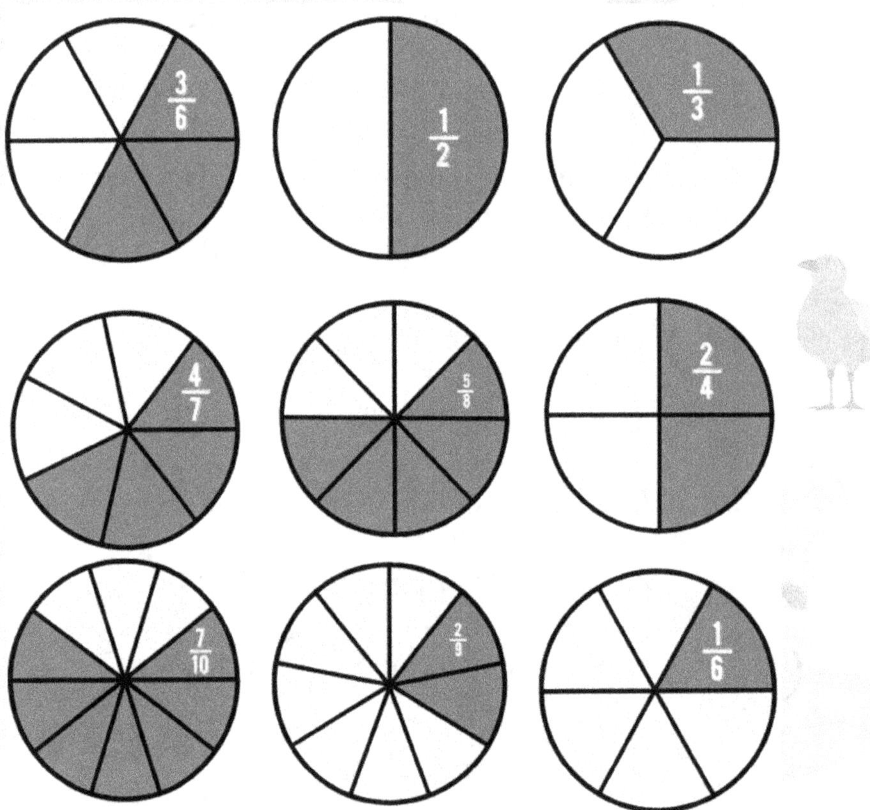

Comparing Fractions

When comparing fractions, we consider the size of their denominators. Generally, the larger the denominator, the smaller the fraction.

For example:

$\frac{1}{3}$ is smaller than $\frac{1}{2}$ because the denominator 3 is larger than the denominator 2.

If the denominators are the same, we can compare the numerators to determine which fraction is larger.

Convert Fractions to Decimals

To transform a fraction into a decimal, we divide the numerator by the denominator.

For instance, $\frac{1}{4}$ equals 0.25 because when we divide 1 by 4, we get 0.25.

In certain cases, the resulting decimal repeats infinitely, like $\frac{1}{3}$, which equals 0.3333... In such instances, we round the decimal to a specific number of decimal places.

Fractions Addition (Common Denominator)

To add fractions with a common denominator, we add their numerators together and keep the denominator the same.

For example: if we want to add $\frac{3}{5}$ and $\frac{2}{5}$ both fractions have the same denominator of 5. Therefore, to add them, we simply add their numerators:

$$\frac{3}{5} + \frac{2}{5} = \frac{3+2}{5} = \frac{5}{5}$$

Fractions Subtraction (Common Denominator)

To subtract fractions with a common denominator, we find the difference between their numerators and keep the denominator the same.

For example:

$$\frac{3}{5} - \frac{2}{5} = \frac{3-2}{5} = \frac{1}{5}$$

<u>Geometry</u>

<u>Area and Perimeter</u>

The area of a shape represents the amount of space it occupies. The perimeter of a shape is the total distance around its outer edge.

Area of Rectangle

For a square, since all four sides are equal, we only need to know the length of one side to find its area. We can calculate the area of a square by multiplying the length of one side by itself (squared). So, if the length of one side of the square is 's', then the area (A) is given by:

$$A = s \times s$$

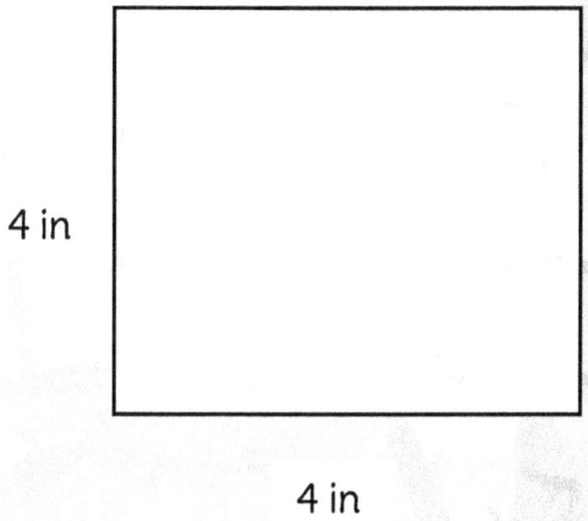

4 in

4 in

$$A = 4 \times 4$$
$$A = 16$$

Perimeter of Rectangle

For a square, since all four sides are equal, we can find the perimeter by adding up the lengths of all four sides. If 's' represents the length of one side, then the perimeter (P) is given by:

$$P = 4 \times s$$

$$P = 4 \times 4$$

$$P = 16$$

Area of Triangle:

The area of a triangle represents the amount of space enclosed within its three sides. The formula for calculating the area of a triangle depends on the type of triangle. For a general triangle, we use the formula:

$$A = \frac{1}{2} \times \text{base} \times \text{height}$$

Where:

- A represents the area of the triangle.

- The base is the length of any one side of the triangle.

- The height is the perpendicular distance from the base to the opposite vertex.

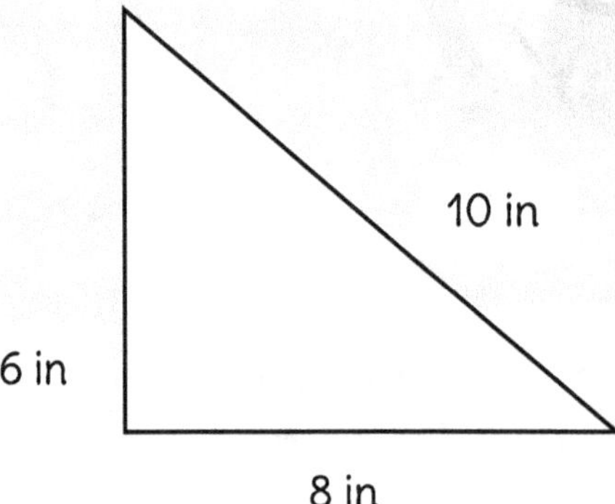

$$A = \frac{1}{2} \times \text{base} \times \text{height}$$

$$A = \frac{1}{2} \times 6 \times 8$$

$$A = \frac{1}{2} \times 48$$

$$A = 24$$

Perimeter of Triangle:

The perimeter of a triangle is the total length of its three sides. To find the perimeter, we simply add the lengths of all three sides together:

$$P = \text{side1} + \text{side2} + \text{side3}$$

$$P = 6 + 8 + 10$$

$$P = 24$$

Equilateral Triangle

An equilateral triangle is a triangle in which all three sides are equal in length. To find the area and perimeter of an equilateral triangle, we can use the following formulas:

- Area (A): $\frac{\sqrt{3}}{4} \times a^2$ where a is the length of one side of the equilateral triangle.
- Perimeter (P): $P = 3a$ where a is the length of one side of the equilateral triangle.

Area of Equilateral Triangle:

$$\text{Area (A): } \frac{\sqrt{3}}{4} \times (6)^2$$

$$\text{Area (A): } \frac{\sqrt{3}}{4} \times 36$$

$$\text{Area (A): } \frac{36\sqrt{3}}{4}$$

$$\text{Area (A): } \frac{36(1.73)}{4}$$

$$\text{Area (A): } \frac{62.35}{4}$$

$$\text{Area (A): } 15.59 \text{ in}^2$$

Perimeter of Equilateral Triangle:

$$P = 3a$$

$$P = 3(6) = 18$$

Unit Conversion

Metric Conversion

1 meter (m) = 100 centimeters (cm)

1 meter (m) = 1000 millimeters (mm)

1 kilometer (km) = 1000 meters (m)

1 hectare (ha) = 10000 square meters (m^2)

1 square meter (m^2) = 10000 square centimeters (cm^2)

1 cubic meter (m^3) = 1000 liters (L)

Weights and Measures

1 kilogram (kg) = 1000 grams (g)

1 liter (L) = 1000 milliliters (mL)

1 tonne (t) = 1000 kilograms (kg)

1 centimeter (cm) = 10 millimeters (mm)

1 gram (g) = 1000 milligrams (mg)

1 kilometer (km) = 100000 centimeters (cm)

Three-Digit Addition

Find the Sum.

1. 429
  + 974
  1,403

2. 296
  + 470
  766

3. 552
  + 154

4. 430
  + 338

5. 769
  + 132

6. 740
  + 205

7. 682
  + 525

8. 872
  + 533

9. 559
  + 523

10. 807
  + 344

11. 965
  + 499

12. 460
  + 688

13. 242
  + 353

14. 454
  + 151

15. 170
  + 516

16. 788
  + 106

17. 836
  + 517

18. 546
  + 766

19. 232
  + 598

20. 599
  + 446

21. 775
  + 932

22. 284
  + 719

23. 338
  + 391

24. 403
  + 276

25. 650
  + 778

26. 633 + 976	**27.** 640 + 594	**28.** 789 + 929	**29.** 614 + 607	**30.** 328 + 298
31. 699 + 379	**32.** 268 + 353	**33.** 343 + 734	**34.** 368 + 265	**35.** 978 + 206
36. 401 + 960	**37.** 923 + 461	**38.** 568 + 133	**39.** 315 + 740	**40.** 450 + 849
41. 949 + 277	**42.** 500 + 391	**43.** 882 + 810	**44.** 465 + 341	**45.** 727 + 616
46. 252 + 624	**47.** 370 + 400	**48.** 746 + 495	**49.** 763 + 929	**50.** 476 + 604

Three-Digit Subtraction

Find the Difference.

1. 790 − 606 = *184*

2. 918 − 550 = *368*

3. 324 − 299

4. 164 − 106

5. 670 − 265

6. 230 − 152

7. 390 − 345

8. 211 − 143

9. 833 − 492

10. 473 − 141

11. 704 − 603

12. 444 − 363

13. 536 − 164

14. 167 − 134

15. 514 − 148

16. 188 − 133

17. 816 − 557

18. 913 − 861

19. 706 − 314

20. 619 − 218

21.	22.	23.	24.	25.
152	257	237	110	969
− 109	− 201	− 205	− 107	− 726

26.	27.	28.	29.	30.
679	326	281	415	158
− 342	− 219	− 269	− 146	− 106

31.	32.	33.	34.	35.
832	669	272	641	947
− 513	− 395	− 232	− 470	− 258

36.	37.	38.	39.	40.
740	961	148	692	649
− 397	− 262	− 124	− 539	− 496

41.	42.	43.	44.	45.
222	586	524	213	493
− 151	− 460	− 388	− 131	− 481

Mixed Two-Digit Practice

Addition and Subtraction

1.
$$994 + 948 = 1{,}942$$

2.
$$240 - 149 = 91$$

3.
$$377 - 157 =$$

4.
$$557 + 111 =$$

5.
$$521 + 686 =$$

6.
$$649 + 945 =$$

7.
$$543 - 479 =$$

8.
$$682 - 195 =$$

9.
$$375 - 255 =$$

10.
$$520 - 333 =$$

11.
$$672 - 542 =$$

12.
$$767 + 850 =$$

13.
$$103 - 102 =$$

14.
$$172 + 771 =$$

15.
$$261 + 842 =$$

16.
$$836 - 438 =$$

17. 894 − 869	**18.** 840 − 148	**19.** 104 + 979	**20.** 358 + 919
21. 487 − 392	**22.** 781 + 347	**23.** 714 − 255	**24.** 387 + 377
25. 808 + 243	**26.** 522 − 121	**27.** 821 − 560	**28.** 589 − 520
29. 733 + 337	**30.** 244 + 779	**31.** 969 − 537	**32.** 170 − 144
33. 510 − 464	**34.** 824 − 488	**35.** 362 + 621	**36.** 575 + 564

37. 350 + 661	**38.** 270 + 309	**39.** 976 + 787	**40.** 732 − 303
41. 475 − 162	**42.** 183 + 367	**43.** 452 + 415	**44.** 535 + 750
45. 755 + 953	**46.** 533 − 112	**47.** 344 − 226	**48.** 314 − 154
49. 164 − 133	**50.** 623 + 916	**51.** 357 + 317	**52.** 582 − 432
53. 798 + 900	**54.** 975 + 477	**55.** 875 − 170	**56.** 691 + 717

Addition with Regrouping

Find the sum.

1. 7,215 + 8,995 **16,210**	**2.** 7,411 + 9,699 **17,110**	**3.** 8,421 + 2,699	**4.** 9,668 + 9,657
5. 6,264 + 9,859	**6.** 3,292 + 8,959	**7.** 4,518 + 9,897	**8.** 8,157 + 8,976
9. 2,639 + 9,589	**10.** 1,443 + 9,688	**11.** 2,588 + 8,635	**12.** 1,731 + 9,689
13. 3,773 + 9,797	**14.** 7,214 + 5,899	**15.** 6,363 + 4,989	**16.** 1,319 + 9,894

17. 4,962 + 6,279	**18.** 4,228 + 8,997	**19.** 1,671 + 9,599	**20.** 7,771 + 4,969
21. 7,729 + 7,985	**22.** 7,423 + 9,787	**23.** 6,859 + 9,756	**24.** 2,128 + 9,995
25. 3,987 + 9,667	**26.** 8,262 + 8,858	**27.** 2,669 + 8,674	**28.** 7,153 + 8,978
29. 7,513 + 6,798	**30.** 6,277 + 8,898	**31.** 5,387 + 5,826	**32.** 4,257 + 7,975
33. 9,125 + 7,987	**34.** 2,692 + 8,488	**35.** 8,241 + 9,899	**36.** 8,235 + 8,875

37. 8,818 + 7,495	**38.** 2,613 + 8,699	**39.** 2,112 + 9,999	**40.** 4,816 + 7,696
41. 8,693 + 7,868	**42.** 2,454 + 8,996	**43.** 6,126 + 9,985	**44.** 4,145 + 8,989
45. 8,883 + 5,457	**46.** 2,397 + 8,926	**47.** 7,919 + 9,891	**48.** 8,639 + 3,583
49. 4,667 + 9,448	**50.** 1,211 + 9,899	**51.** 8,433 + 3,797	**52.** 2,753 + 9,859
53. 1,832 + 9,899	**54.** 9,339 + 5,883	**55.** 1,111 + 9,999	**56.** 7,758 + 6,892

Subtraction with Regrouping

Find the difference.

1. $9{,}202 - 5{,}533 = 3{,}669$	**2.** $5{,}606 - 2{,}869$	**3.** $4{,}406 - 3{,}939$

1. 9,202 − 5,533 = 3,669

2. 5,606 − 2,869

3. 4,406 − 3,939

4. 4,208 − 3,649

5. 2,103 − 1,564

6. 6,202 − 1,693

7. 7,207 − 3,348

8. 2,602 − 1,765

9. 6,803 − 3,918

10. 3,308 − 2,459

11. 6,808 − 2,949

12. 3,406 − 2,577

13. 9,805 − 8,978

14. 8,302 − 5,976

15. 6,100 − 1,855

16. 3,807 − 1,979

17.	7,702 − 6,926	18.	7,304 − 6,695	19.	4,206 − 2,817	20.	2,301 − 1,838
21.	9,605 − 7,858	22.	3,204 − 2,555	23.	4,801 − 1,937	24.	8,303 − 7,779
25.	2,607 − 1,929	26.	8,705 − 2,868	27.	4,807 − 2,979	28.	4,806 − 3,958
29.	4,507 − 3,978	30.	3,300 − 1,992	31.	8,008 − 6,699	32.	2,801 − 1,993
33.	3,507 − 1,789	34.	5,405 − 4,718	35.	7,008 − 1,989	36.	6,006 − 1,458

37. $\begin{array}{r} 2{,}701 \\ -\ 1{,}873 \\ \hline \end{array}$	**38.** $\begin{array}{r} 6{,}805 \\ -\ 5{,}916 \\ \hline \end{array}$	**39.** $\begin{array}{r} 2{,}004 \\ -\ 1{,}416 \\ \hline \end{array}$	**40.** $\begin{array}{r} 3{,}805 \\ -\ 2{,}978 \\ \hline \end{array}$
41. $\begin{array}{r} 3{,}208 \\ -\ 2{,}359 \\ \hline \end{array}$	**42.** $\begin{array}{r} 4{,}200 \\ -\ 2{,}371 \\ \hline \end{array}$	**43.** $\begin{array}{r} 2{,}508 \\ -\ 1{,}759 \\ \hline \end{array}$	**44.** $\begin{array}{r} 8{,}608 \\ -\ 3{,}939 \\ \hline \end{array}$
45. $\begin{array}{r} 5{,}805 \\ -\ 1{,}957 \\ \hline \end{array}$	**46.** $\begin{array}{r} 6{,}603 \\ -\ 3{,}799 \\ \hline \end{array}$	**47.** $\begin{array}{r} 3{,}703 \\ -\ 2{,}944 \\ \hline \end{array}$	**48.** $\begin{array}{r} 3{,}806 \\ -\ 1{,}917 \\ \hline \end{array}$
49. $\begin{array}{r} 6{,}801 \\ -\ 1{,}994 \\ \hline \end{array}$	**50.** $\begin{array}{r} 6{,}203 \\ -\ 1{,}668 \\ \hline \end{array}$	**51.** $\begin{array}{r} 6{,}702 \\ -\ 1{,}944 \\ \hline \end{array}$	**52.** $\begin{array}{r} 2{,}602 \\ -\ 1{,}737 \\ \hline \end{array}$
53. $\begin{array}{r} 6{,}106 \\ -\ 4{,}928 \\ \hline \end{array}$	**54.** $\begin{array}{r} 9{,}804 \\ -\ 3{,}979 \\ \hline \end{array}$	**55.** $\begin{array}{r} 8{,}300 \\ -\ 4{,}975 \\ \hline \end{array}$	**56.** $\begin{array}{r} 6{,}701 \\ -\ 5{,}933 \\ \hline \end{array}$

Three-Addends

Find the sum.

1.	2.	3.	4.
155	154	763	633
593	578	206	423
+ 839	+ 357	+ 206	+ 510
1,587			

5.	6.	7.	8.
693	865	387	755
641	943	873	518
+ 494	+ 728	+ 130	+ 170

9.	10.	11.	12.
589	664	192	163
645	498	584	957
+ 393	+ 755	+ 760	+ 570

13. 216 838 + 133	**14.** 152 199 + 649	**15.** 671 717 + 716	**16.** 356 472 + 209
17. 205 399 + 350	**18.** 789 902 + 513	**19.** 441 398 + 175	**20.** 768 564 + 931
21. 963 199 + 707	**22.** 449 541 + 838	**23.** 750 630 + 683	**24.** 923 748 + 205
25. 694 335 + 774	**26.** 480 184 + 799	**27.** 453 334 + 273	**28.** 284 559 + 199

29.	30.	31.	32.
506	346	495	201
402	721	447	188
+ 682	+ 658	+ 374	+ 999

33.	34.	35.	36.
941	877	525	244
322	605	281	195
+ 276	+ 841	+ 650	+ 667

37.	38.	39.	40.
739	375	758	608
960	415	779	942
+ 314	+ 330	+ 640	+ 239

41.	42.	43.	44.
256	125	830	774
503	528	594	539
+ 909	+ 402	+ 247	+ 862

Place Value

Determine the place value of the underlined digit.

1. 6̲0,034 = 6 ten thousands

2. 2̲5,768 = 5 thousands

3. 29,74̲9 =

4. 57,1̲21 =

5. 2̲6,251 =

6. 1̲5,773 =

7. 2̲7,920 =

8. 3̲6,716 =

9. 2̲8,538 =

10. 46,7̲81 =

11. 9̲1,926 =

12. 78,2̲96 =

13. 31̲,441 =

14. 37,16̲8 =

15. 91̲,689 =

16. 94,25̲5 =

17. 69,665 = _______________

18. 64,452 = _______________

19. 41,647 = _______________

20. 31,097 = _______________

21. 36,925 = _______________

22. 87,013 = _______________

23. 27,649 = _______________

24. 62,917 = _______________

25. 95,744 = _______________

26. 54,197 = _______________

27. 37,234 = _______________

28. 69,003 = _______________

29. 23,931 = _______________

30. 77,784 = _______________

31. 95,649 = _______________

32. 73,197 = _______________

Place Value: Expanded Notation

Provide the expanded notation for each value.

1. 86,629   eighty-six thousand six hundred twenty-nine

2. _______________ fifty-nine thousand one hundred nineteen

3. _______________ ninety-two thousand seven hundred seventy-seven

4. _______________ eighty-six thousand five hundred ninety-nine

5. _______________ thirty-five thousand five

6. _______________ sixty-six thousand six hundred twelve

7. _______________ twenty thousand eight hundred nine

8. _______________ sixty-six thousand seven hundred forty-three

9. _______________ twenty-five thousand eight hundred forty

10. _______________ ninety-three thousand seven hundred sixty-six

11. _______________ fifty-two thousand eight hundred nine

12. _______________ eleven thousand four hundred eighty-nine

13. _______________ thirty-six thousand one hundred five

14. _______________ sixty-eight thousand seven hundred sixty-eight

15. _______________ fifty-seven thousand eight hundred sixty-four

16. _______________ twenty-six thousand thirty-two

17. _______________ thirty-three thousand nine hundred

18. ___________________ eleven thousand nine hundred

19. ___________________ eighty thousand eight hundred seventy-five

20. ___________________ ninety-four thousand nine hundred sixty-eight

21. ___________________ seventy-three thousand eighty-four

22. ___________________ forty-four thousand ninety-two

23. ___________________ forty-five thousand three hundred ninety-three

24. ___________________ twenty-four thousand one hundred fifty-one

25. ___________________ seventy-eight thousand one hundred sixty-five

26. ___________________ seventy-seven thousand nine hundred seventy-five

27. _____________ ninety-two thousand eight hundred ninety-eight

28. _____________ seventy-one thousand eight hundred sixty-three

29. _____________ thirty-two thousand three hundred four

30. _____________ ninety-six thousand six hundred eighty

31. _____________ ninety-nine thousand two hundred eighteen

32. _____________ ninety-seven thousand four hundred ninety-three

33. _____________ ninety thousand six hundred twenty-two

34. _____________ thirty-three thousand thirty-nine

35. _____________ forty thousand five hundred seventy-eight

36. _______________ seventy-eight thousand six hundred fifty

37. _______________ fifty thousand four hundred eighty-six

38. _______________ nineteen thousand four hundred thirty-seven

39. _______________ twenty-one thousand three hundred

40. _______________ seventy-two thousand four hundred ninety-eight

41. _______________ thirty-eight thousand five hundred seventy-eight

42. _______________ twenty-two thousand eight hundred eighty-three

43. _______________ thirty-five thousand seven hundred sixty-four

Multiplication: 2 x 1

Find the product.

1.
$$20 \times 4 = 80$$

2.
$$13 \times 3$$

3.
$$11 \times 2$$

4.
$$12 \times 4$$

5.
$$23 \times 2$$

6.
$$18 \times 1$$

7.
$$40 \times 2$$

8.
$$33 \times 2$$

9.
$$85 \times 1$$

10.
$$10 \times 5$$

11.
$$31 \times 2$$

12.
$$13 \times 2$$

13.
$$12 \times 2$$

14.
$$10 \times 4$$

15.
$$11 \times 4$$

16.
$$31 \times 3$$

17.   23
× 3

18.   11
× 3

19.   22
× 4

20.   21
× 4

21.   12
× 3

22.   30
× 2

23.   34
× 2

24.   21
× 2

25.   30
× 3

26.   32
× 3

27.   10
× 2

28.   21
× 3

29.   14
× 2

30.   51
× 1

31.   32
× 2

32.   55
× 1

33.   22
× 3

34.   62
× 1

35.   11
× 5

36.   22
× 2

Multiplication: 3 x 1

Find the product.

1. 111 × 3 333	**2.** 320 × 3	**3.** 121 × 4

1. 111
    × 3
    333

2. 320
    × 3

3. 121
    × 4

4. 110
    × 5

5. 230
    × 3

6. 101
    × 5

7. 131
    × 3

8. 100
    × 4

9. 201
    × 4

10. 304
    × 2

11. 132
    × 3

12. 211
    × 4

13. 302
    × 3

14. 220
    × 4

15. 311
    × 3

16. 122
    × 4

17.
$$\begin{array}{r} 222 \\ \times\ \ 4 \\ \hline \end{array}$$

18.
$$\begin{array}{r} 201 \\ \times\ \ 2 \\ \hline \end{array}$$

19.
$$\begin{array}{r} 414 \\ \times\ \ 2 \\ \hline \end{array}$$

20.
$$\begin{array}{r} 223 \\ \times\ \ 3 \\ \hline \end{array}$$

21.
$$\begin{array}{r} 300 \\ \times\ \ 2 \\ \hline \end{array}$$

22.
$$\begin{array}{r} 111 \\ \times\ \ 4 \\ \hline \end{array}$$

23.
$$\begin{array}{r} 353 \\ \times\ \ 1 \\ \hline \end{array}$$

24.
$$\begin{array}{r} 241 \\ \times\ \ 2 \\ \hline \end{array}$$

25.
$$\begin{array}{r} 330 \\ \times\ \ 3 \\ \hline \end{array}$$

26.
$$\begin{array}{r} 231 \\ \times\ \ 3 \\ \hline \end{array}$$

27.
$$\begin{array}{r} 232 \\ \times\ \ 3 \\ \hline \end{array}$$

28.
$$\begin{array}{r} 433 \\ \times\ \ 2 \\ \hline \end{array}$$

29.
$$\begin{array}{r} 101 \\ \times\ \ 4 \\ \hline \end{array}$$

30.
$$\begin{array}{r} 211 \\ \times\ \ 2 \\ \hline \end{array}$$

31.
$$\begin{array}{r} 213 \\ \times\ \ 2 \\ \hline \end{array}$$

32.
$$\begin{array}{r} 402 \\ \times\ \ 2 \\ \hline \end{array}$$

33.
$$\begin{array}{r} 313 \\ \times\ \ 3 \\ \hline \end{array}$$

34.
$$\begin{array}{r} 332 \\ \times\ \ 2 \\ \hline \end{array}$$

35.
$$\begin{array}{r} 123 \\ \times\ \ 3 \\ \hline \end{array}$$

36.
$$\begin{array}{r} 300 \\ \times\ \ 3 \\ \hline \end{array}$$

Multiplication: 4 x 1

Find the product.

1.
$$\begin{array}{r} 1{,}211 \\ \times\ \ \ \ 2 \\ \hline 2422 \end{array}$$

2.
$$\begin{array}{r} 1{,}322 \\ \times\ \ \ \ 2 \\ \hline \end{array}$$

3.
$$\begin{array}{r} 2{,}212 \\ \times\ \ \ \ 3 \\ \hline \end{array}$$

4.
$$\begin{array}{r} 3{,}100 \\ \times\ \ \ \ 3 \\ \hline \end{array}$$

5.
$$\begin{array}{r} 3{,}232 \\ \times\ \ \ \ 3 \\ \hline \end{array}$$

6.
$$\begin{array}{r} 2{,}200 \\ \times\ \ \ \ 4 \\ \hline \end{array}$$

7.
$$\begin{array}{r} 2{,}003 \\ \times\ \ \ \ 3 \\ \hline \end{array}$$

8.
$$\begin{array}{r} 3{,}220 \\ \times\ \ \ \ 3 \\ \hline \end{array}$$

9.
$$\begin{array}{r} 4{,}411 \\ \times\ \ \ \ 2 \\ \hline \end{array}$$

10.
$$\begin{array}{r} 3{,}004 \\ \times\ \ \ \ 2 \\ \hline \end{array}$$

11.
$$\begin{array}{r} 1{,}212 \\ \times\ \ \ \ 2 \\ \hline \end{array}$$

12.
$$\begin{array}{r} 1{,}010 \\ \times\ \ \ \ 5 \\ \hline \end{array}$$

13.
$$\begin{array}{r} 3{,}122 \\ \times\ \ \ \ 2 \\ \hline \end{array}$$

14.
$$\begin{array}{r} 1{,}404 \\ \times\ \ \ \ 2 \\ \hline \end{array}$$

15.
$$\begin{array}{r} 5{,}373 \\ \times\ \ \ \ 1 \\ \hline \end{array}$$

16.
$$\begin{array}{r} 1{,}233 \\ \times\ \ \ \ 3 \\ \hline \end{array}$$

17.
$$2{,}021 \times 3$$

18.
$$3{,}124 \times 2$$

19.
$$1{,}011 \times 5$$

20.
$$1{,}100 \times 4$$

21.
$$1{,}222 \times 4$$

22.
$$2{,}201 \times 2$$

23.
$$3{,}322 \times 3$$

24.
$$1{,}111 \times 4$$

25.
$$2{,}203 \times 2$$

26.
$$1{,}102 \times 4$$

27.
$$4{,}323 \times 2$$

28.
$$1{,}101 \times 4$$

29.
$$3{,}222 \times 3$$

30.
$$4{,}113 \times 2$$

31.
$$1{,}022 \times 4$$

32.
$$2{,}433 \times 2$$

33.
$$3{,}423 \times 2$$

34.
$$4{,}000 \times 2$$

35.
$$2{,}223 \times 3$$

36.
$$1{,}224 \times 2$$

Multiplication (double Digit)

Find the product.

1.
$$34 \times 58$$

2.
$$12 \times 47$$

3.
$$44 \times 70$$

4.
$$72 \times 45$$

5.
$$42 \times 56$$

6.
$$42 \times 16$$

7.
$$90 \times 62$$

8.
$$78 \times 17$$

9.
$$96 \times 61$$

10.
$$87 \times 45$$

11.
$$81 \times 32$$

12.
$$35 \times 79$$

13. $\begin{array}{r} 61 \\ \times\ 85 \\ \hline \end{array}$	**14.** $\begin{array}{r} 80 \\ \times\ 29 \\ \hline \end{array}$	**15.** $\begin{array}{r} 74 \\ \times\ 65 \\ \hline \end{array}$	**16.** $\begin{array}{r} 16 \\ \times\ 91 \\ \hline \end{array}$
17. $\begin{array}{r} 35 \\ \times\ 98 \\ \hline \end{array}$	**18.** $\begin{array}{r} 83 \\ \times\ 75 \\ \hline \end{array}$	**19.** $\begin{array}{r} 65 \\ \times\ 73 \\ \hline \end{array}$	**20.** $\begin{array}{r} 67 \\ \times\ 13 \\ \hline \end{array}$
21. $\begin{array}{r} 85 \\ \times\ 81 \\ \hline \end{array}$	**22.** $\begin{array}{r} 13 \\ \times\ 22 \\ \hline \end{array}$	**23.** $\begin{array}{r} 25 \\ \times\ 40 \\ \hline \end{array}$	**24.** $\begin{array}{r} 73 \\ \times\ 25 \\ \hline \end{array}$

25. $\begin{array}{r} 20 \\ \times\ 27 \\ \hline \end{array}$	**26.** $\begin{array}{r} 62 \\ \times\ 46 \\ \hline \end{array}$	**27.** $\begin{array}{r} 84 \\ \times\ 90 \\ \hline \end{array}$	**28.** $\begin{array}{r} 15 \\ \times\ 12 \\ \hline \end{array}$
29. $\begin{array}{r} 33 \\ \times\ 32 \\ \hline \end{array}$	**30.** $\begin{array}{r} 85 \\ \times\ 58 \\ \hline \end{array}$	**31.** $\begin{array}{r} 89 \\ \times\ 53 \\ \hline \end{array}$	**32.** $\begin{array}{r} 69 \\ \times\ 76 \\ \hline \end{array}$
33. $\begin{array}{r} 50 \\ \times\ 50 \\ \hline \end{array}$	**34.** $\begin{array}{r} 79 \\ \times\ 91 \\ \hline \end{array}$	**35.** $\begin{array}{r} 77 \\ \times\ 12 \\ \hline \end{array}$	**36.** $\begin{array}{r} 51 \\ \times\ 34 \\ \hline \end{array}$

37.	38.	39.	40.
93 × 84	59 × 99	29 × 23	64 × 31

41.	42.	43.	44.
22 × 65	19 × 57	13 × 69	16 × 45

45.	46.	47.	48.
93 × 82	52 × 43	87 × 19	23 × 42

Basic Division

Find the quotient.

1. $2\overline{)8}$ 4

2. $7\overline{)49}$

3. $6\overline{)48}$

4. $5\overline{)10}$

5. $8\overline{)32}$

6. $5\overline{)5}$

7. $4\overline{)4}$

8. $8\overline{)16}$

9. $7\overline{)42}$

10. $5\overline{)15}$

11. $4\overline{)8}$

12. $7\overline{)56}$

13. $4\overline{)16}$

14. $10\overline{)100}$

15. $6\overline{)12}$

16. $5\overline{)40}$

17.

$7 \overline{)21}$

18.

$9 \overline{)81}$

19.

$5 \overline{)45}$

20.

$7 \overline{)28}$

21.

$3 \overline{)3}$

22.

$8 \overline{)56}$

23.

$3 \overline{)6}$

24.

$1 \overline{)9}$

25.

$1 \overline{)4}$

26.

$8 \overline{)24}$

27.

$7 \overline{)63}$

28.

$10 \overline{)10}$

29.

$6 \overline{)54}$

30.

$4 \overline{)12}$

31.

$8 \overline{)40}$

32.

$6 \overline{)42}$

33.

$9 \overline{)63}$

34.

$3 \overline{)27}$

35.

$9 \overline{)18}$

36.

$4 \overline{)40}$

37.

$6\overline{)24}$

38.

$9\overline{)27}$

39.

$2\overline{)16}$

40.

$4\overline{)24}$

41.

$6\overline{)30}$

42.

$8\overline{)48}$

43.

$8\overline{)72}$

44.

$7\overline{)14}$

45.

$7\overline{)7}$

46.

$4\overline{)28}$

47.

$3\overline{)24}$

48.

$6\overline{)36}$

49.

$9\overline{)36}$

50.

$2\overline{)10}$

51.

$5\overline{)20}$

52.

$10\overline{)70}$

53.

$3\overline{)21}$

54.

$3\overline{)18}$

55.

$9\overline{)9}$

56.

$2\overline{)6}$

Long Division

Find the quotient.

1.
$$12\overline{)444}$$
(answer: 37)

2.
$$7\overline{)434}$$

3.
$$10\overline{)880}$$

4.
$$2\overline{)100}$$

5.
$$9\overline{)486}$$

6.
$$6\overline{)192}$$

7.
$$6\overline{)252}$$

8.
$$5\overline{)350}$$

9.
$$10\overline{)930}$$

10.
$$12\overline{)24}$$

11.
$$7\overline{)217}$$

12.
$$3\overline{)255}$$

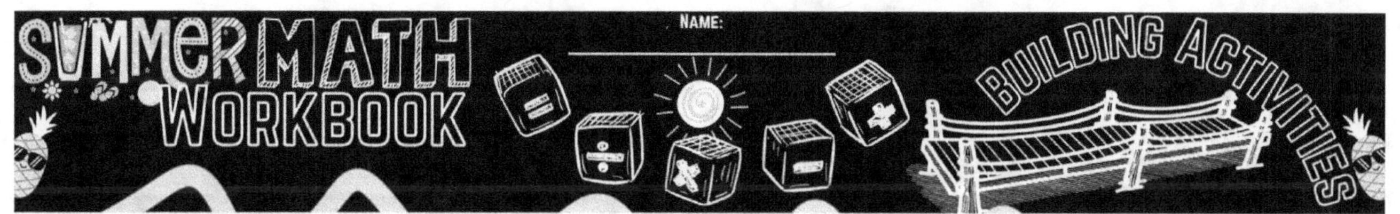

13.

11⟌682

14.

10⟌730

15.

2⟌146

16.

4⟌68

17.

12⟌396

18.

6⟌24

19.

4⟌348

20.

7⟌658

21.

5⟌240

22.

11⟌715

23.

4⟌368

24.

2⟌48

25.

6⟌312

26.

4⟌388

27.

2⟌12

28.

9⟌621

29.

$3\overline{)216}$

30.

$9\overline{)216}$

31.

$2\overline{)78}$

32.

$5\overline{)5}$

33.

$4\overline{)112}$

34.

$5\overline{)75}$

35.

$12\overline{)360}$

36.

$6\overline{)594}$

37.

$6\overline{)12}$

38.

$8\overline{)56}$

39.

$6\overline{)300}$

40.

$7\overline{)665}$

41.

$7\overline{)399}$

42.

$4\overline{)236}$

43.

$6\overline{)168}$

44.

$2\overline{)182}$

Adding Decimals

Find the sum.

1.
655.58
+ 782.39
1,437.97

2.
826.63
+ 574.45

3.
209.90
+ 342.75

4.
881.57
+ 102.76

5.
172.77
+ 893.17

6.
425.35
+ 106.14

7.
608.03
+ 955.54

8.
339.16
+ 276.21

9.
159.68
+ 367.94

10.
583.22
+ 145.23

11.
480.31
+ 679.69

12.
336.32
+ 754.96

13. 234.62
   + 819.44
   ____

14. 739.12
   + 559.98
   ____

15. 229.03
   + 834.31
   ____

16. 600.84
   + 110.81
   ____

17. 252.66
   + 504.86
   ____

18. 571.09
   + 289.92
   ____

19. 534.96
   + 932.71
   ____

20. 880.86
   + 245.61
   ____

21. 230.21
   + 661.16
   ____

22. 979.04
   + 586.19
   ____

23. 220.51
   + 608.66
   ____

24. 444.26
   + 613.36
   ____

25. 369.07
+ 138.46
____

26. 564.53
+ 231.82
____

27. 765.26
+ 144.34
____

28. 534.57
+ 975.74
____

29. 546.14
+ 171.60
____

30. 439.88
+ 390.35
____

31. 603.65
+ 421.51
____

32. 873.72
+ 338.35
____

33. 392.40
+ 414.51
____

34. 853.47
+ 203.11
____

35. 484.54
+ 149.22
____

36. 741.25
+ 226.87
____

Subtracting Decimals

Find the difference.

1.	989.80 − 136.41 **853.39**	**2.**	299.18 − 251.18	**3.**	669.18 − 457.77
4.	528.33 − 127.36	**5.**	287.97 − 285.86	**6.**	707.90 − 317.81
7.	782.94 − 518.62	**8.**	343.96 − 330.49	**9.**	670.46 − 556.74
10.	626.89 − 100.52	**11.**	227.27 − 154.14	**12.**	616.99 − 182.80

13. 755.27 − 723.88	**14.** 907.81 − 423.00	**15.** 865.24 − 810.18
16. 749.86 − 233.95	**17.** 848.68 − 109.80	**18.** 461.37 − 114.45
19. 777.85 − 653.85	**20.** 239.17 − 159.15	**21.** 828.01 − 748.41
22. 720.65 − 533.76	**23.** 806.87 − 533.87	**24.** 929.26 − 300.03

25. 939.60
− 111.34

26. 637.08
− 602.86

27. 448.90
− 292.67

28. 986.27
− 196.10

29. 533.12
− 366.54

30. 693.96
− 314.08

31. 724.10
− 466.10

32. 885.07
− 183.06

33. 771.87
− 280.56

34. 793.13
− 672.54

35. 350.66
− 149.43

36. 470.55
− 202.81

Fraction Identification

Identify fractions of each set of boxes.

1. 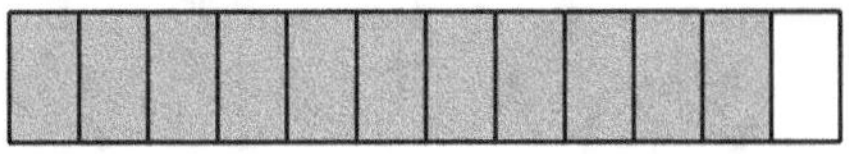 $= \dfrac{11}{12}$

____

2. 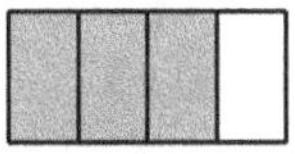 =

____

3. 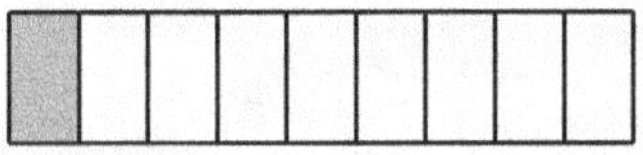 =

____

4. 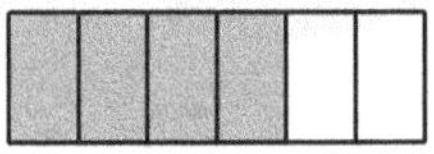 =

____

5.  =

____

6. 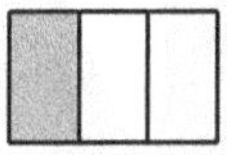 =

____

7. 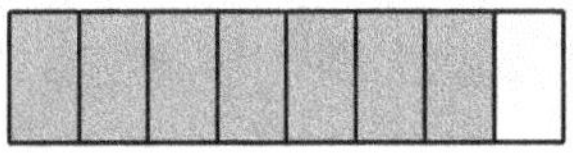 =

____

8. =
____

9. =
____

10. =
____

11. =
____

12. =
____

13. =
____

14. =
____

15. =
____

16. ________________________ =

____

17. ________________________ =

____

18. ________ =

____

19. ____________ =

____

20. ____________ =

____

21. ________________________________ =

____

22. ________ =

____

23. ____________________ =

____

24. =

____

25. =

____

26. =

____

27. =

____

28. =

____

29. =

____

30. =

____

31. =

____

32. 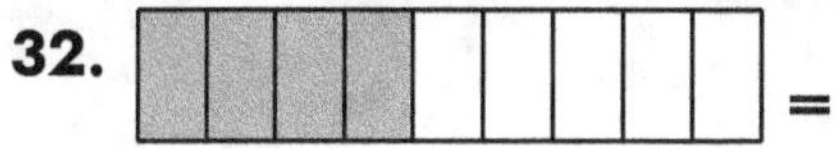 =

____

33. =

____

34.  =

____

35. =

____

36. =

____

37.  =

____

38. =

____

39. =

____

Compare the Fractions

Put the signs < , >, or =

1. $\dfrac{56}{84}$ < $\dfrac{183}{84}$

2. $\dfrac{14}{13}$ __ $\dfrac{2}{13}$

3. $\dfrac{35}{40}$ __ $\dfrac{7}{40}$

4. $\dfrac{25}{40}$ __ $\dfrac{39}{40}$

5. $\dfrac{49}{36}$ __ $\dfrac{50}{36}$

6. $\dfrac{10}{48}$ __ $\dfrac{33}{48}$

7. $\dfrac{17}{9}$ __ $\dfrac{8}{9}$

8. $\dfrac{15}{30}$ __ $\dfrac{69}{30}$

9. $\dfrac{9}{14}$ __ $\dfrac{16}{14}$

10. $\dfrac{26}{10}$ __ $\dfrac{28}{10}$

11. $\dfrac{83}{32}$ __ $\dfrac{28}{32}$

12. $\dfrac{22}{44}$ __ $\dfrac{110}{44}$

13. $\dfrac{1}{2}$ ___ $\dfrac{1}{2}$

14. $\dfrac{10}{64}$ ___ $\dfrac{178}{64}$

15. $\dfrac{61}{23}$ ___ $\dfrac{21}{23}$

16. $\dfrac{4}{13}$ ___ $\dfrac{2}{13}$

17. $\dfrac{1}{3}$ ___ $\dfrac{8}{3}$

18. $\dfrac{18}{7}$ ___ $\dfrac{5}{7}$

19. $\dfrac{62}{70}$ ___ $\dfrac{61}{70}$

20. $\dfrac{47}{24}$ ___ $\dfrac{50}{24}$

21. $\dfrac{56}{200}$ ___ $\dfrac{167}{200}$

22. $\dfrac{12}{17}$ ___ $\dfrac{7}{17}$

23. $\dfrac{28}{56}$ ___ $\dfrac{49}{56}$

24. $\dfrac{37}{16}$ ___ $\dfrac{5}{16}$

25. $\dfrac{43}{15}$ ___ $\dfrac{35}{15}$

26. $\dfrac{24}{32}$ ___ $\dfrac{29}{32}$

27. $\dfrac{66}{80}$ ___ $\dfrac{14}{80}$

28. $\dfrac{5}{9}$ ___ $\dfrac{3}{9}$

29. $\dfrac{9}{5}$ ___ $\dfrac{4}{5}$

30. $\dfrac{93}{100}$ ___ $\dfrac{13}{100}$

31. $\dfrac{46}{72}$ ___ $\dfrac{38}{72}$

32. $\dfrac{43}{18}$ ___ $\dfrac{14}{18}$

33. $\dfrac{57}{20}$ ___ $\dfrac{19}{20}$

34. $\dfrac{12}{90}$ ___ $\dfrac{28}{90}$

35. $\dfrac{81}{60}$ ___ $\dfrac{49}{60}$

36. $\dfrac{3}{6}$ ___ $\dfrac{4}{6}$

37. $\dfrac{74}{75}$ ___ $\dfrac{6}{75}$

38. $\dfrac{18}{11}$ ___ $\dfrac{13}{11}$

39. $\dfrac{43}{21}$ ___ $\dfrac{18}{21}$

40. $\dfrac{63}{25}$ ___ $\dfrac{6}{25}$

Convert Fractions to Decimals

Write decimal equivalent of the fractions.

1. $\dfrac{98}{100} =$ ___________________

2. $\dfrac{8}{13} =$ ___________________

3. $\dfrac{2}{5} =$ ___________________

4. $\dfrac{29}{50} =$ ___________________

5. $\dfrac{6}{13} =$ ___________________

6. $\dfrac{6}{23} =$ ___________________

7. $\dfrac{4}{25} =$ ___________________

8. $\dfrac{2}{7} =$ ___________________

9. $\dfrac{64}{70} =$ ___________________

10. $\dfrac{12}{100} =$ ___________________

11. $\dfrac{1}{2}$ = _______________

12. $\dfrac{8}{17}$ = _______________

13. $\dfrac{1}{5}$ = _______________

14. $\dfrac{6}{8}$ = _______________

15. $\dfrac{6}{18}$ = _______________

16. $\dfrac{7}{10}$ = _______________

17. $\dfrac{5}{9}$ = _______________

18. $\dfrac{13}{16}$ = _______________

19. $\dfrac{57}{75}$ = _______________

20. $\dfrac{15}{21}$ = _______________

21. $\dfrac{36}{50}$ = _______________

22. $\dfrac{5}{30}$ = _______________

23. $\dfrac{2}{12} =$ _______________________

24. $\dfrac{18}{20} =$ _______________________

25. $\dfrac{1}{3} =$ _______________________

26. $\dfrac{1}{6} =$ _______________________

27. $\dfrac{7}{15} =$ _______________________

28. $\dfrac{10}{14} =$ _______________________

29. $\dfrac{18}{36} =$ _______________________

30. $\dfrac{9}{11} =$ _______________________

31. $\dfrac{21}{24} =$ _______________________

32. $\dfrac{1}{4} =$ _______________________

33. $\dfrac{3}{19} =$ _______________________

34. $\dfrac{9}{22} =$ _______________________

Fractions Addition (Common Denominator)

Find the sum.

1. $\frac{2}{6} + \frac{1}{6} =$ _______________

2. $\frac{2}{10} + \frac{4}{10} =$ _______________

3. $\frac{1}{4} + \frac{2}{4} =$ _______________

4. $\frac{8}{12} + \frac{1}{12} =$ _______________

5. $\frac{1}{2} + \frac{1}{2} =$ _______________

6. $\frac{3}{9} + \frac{2}{9} =$ _______________

7. $\frac{2}{5} + \frac{1}{5} =$ _______________

8. $\frac{1}{3} + \frac{1}{3} =$ _______________

9. $\frac{1}{6} + \frac{4}{6} =$ _______________

10. $\frac{3}{10} + \frac{3}{10} =$ _______________

11. $\frac{2}{8} + \frac{1}{8} =$ _______________

12. $\frac{3}{7} + \frac{3}{7} =$ _______________

13. $\dfrac{1}{11} + \dfrac{1}{11} =$ _______________

14. $\dfrac{7}{12} + \dfrac{2}{12} =$ _______________

15. $\dfrac{1}{5} + \dfrac{2}{5} =$ _______________

16. $\dfrac{6}{9} + \dfrac{1}{9} =$ _______________

17. $\dfrac{2}{11} + \dfrac{8}{11} =$ _______________

18. $\dfrac{5}{8} + \dfrac{1}{8} =$ _______________

19. $\dfrac{1}{4} + \dfrac{1}{4} =$ _______________

20. $\dfrac{1}{10} + \dfrac{7}{10} =$ _______________

21. $\dfrac{3}{7} + \dfrac{2}{7} =$ _______________

22. $\dfrac{2}{6} + \dfrac{2}{6} =$ _______________

23. $\dfrac{9}{12} + \dfrac{2}{12} =$ _______________

24. $\dfrac{4}{8} + \dfrac{3}{8} =$ _______________

25. $\dfrac{1}{5} + \dfrac{3}{5} =$ _______________

26. $\dfrac{4}{11} + \dfrac{6}{11} =$ _______________

27. $\dfrac{4}{9} + \dfrac{2}{9} =$ _______________

28. $\dfrac{4}{10} + \dfrac{1}{10} =$ _______________

29. $\dfrac{3}{6} + \dfrac{1}{6} =$ _______________

30. $\dfrac{1}{7} + \dfrac{5}{7} =$ _______________

31. $\dfrac{1}{11} + \dfrac{5}{11} =$ _______________

32. $\dfrac{2}{8} + \dfrac{4}{8} =$ _______________

33. $\dfrac{2}{5} + \dfrac{2}{5} =$ _______________

34. $\dfrac{5}{12} + \dfrac{2}{12} =$ _______________

35. $\dfrac{2}{10} + \dfrac{6}{10} =$ _______________

36. $\dfrac{2}{12} + \dfrac{4}{12} =$ _______________

37. $\dfrac{4}{9} + \dfrac{1}{9} =$ _______________

38. $\dfrac{2}{8} + \dfrac{2}{8} =$ _______________

39. $\dfrac{2}{4} + \dfrac{1}{4} =$ _______________

40. $\dfrac{4}{11} + \dfrac{2}{11} =$ _______________

41. $\dfrac{6}{12} + \dfrac{5}{12} =$ _______________

42. $\dfrac{2}{11} + \dfrac{3}{11} =$ _______________

43. $\dfrac{2}{7} + \dfrac{2}{7} =$ _______________

44. $\dfrac{1}{6} + \dfrac{3}{6} =$ _______________

45. $\dfrac{1}{10} + \dfrac{6}{10} =$ _______________

46. $\dfrac{1}{9} + \dfrac{2}{9} =$ _______________

47. $\dfrac{1}{5} + \dfrac{1}{5} =$ _______________

48. $\dfrac{5}{7} + \dfrac{1}{7} =$ _______________

49. $\dfrac{1}{12} + \dfrac{4}{12} =$ _______________

50. $\dfrac{2}{11} + \dfrac{2}{11} =$ _______________

51. $\dfrac{3}{8} + \dfrac{2}{8} =$ _______________

52. $\dfrac{1}{9} + \dfrac{4}{9} =$ _______________

53. $\dfrac{6}{11} + \dfrac{3}{11} =$ _______________

54. $\dfrac{2}{8} + \dfrac{5}{8} =$ _______________

55. $\dfrac{3}{9} + \dfrac{4}{9} =$ _______________

56. $\dfrac{1}{6} + \dfrac{1}{6} =$ _______________

57. $\dfrac{5}{10} + \dfrac{4}{10} =$ _______________

58. $\dfrac{6}{12} + \dfrac{4}{12} =$ _______________

59. $\dfrac{7}{9} + \dfrac{1}{9} =$ _______________

60. $\dfrac{2}{10} + \dfrac{1}{10} =$ _______________

Fractions Subtraction: (Common Denominator)

Find the difference.

1. $\dfrac{6}{7} - \dfrac{4}{7} =$ _______________

2. $\dfrac{2}{3} - \dfrac{1}{3} =$ _______________

3. $\dfrac{3}{5} - \dfrac{1}{5} =$ _______________

4. $\dfrac{5}{6} - \dfrac{1}{6} =$ _______________

5. $\dfrac{3}{9} - \dfrac{2}{9} =$ _______________

6. $\dfrac{7}{10} - \dfrac{6}{10} =$ _______________

7. $\dfrac{4}{5} - \dfrac{3}{5} =$ _______________

8. $\dfrac{2}{6} - \dfrac{1}{6} =$ _______________

9. $\dfrac{8}{12} - \dfrac{7}{12} =$ _______________

10. $\dfrac{6}{7} - \dfrac{5}{7} =$ _______________

11. $\dfrac{7}{8} - \dfrac{2}{8} =$ _______________

12. $\dfrac{8}{9} - \dfrac{7}{9} =$ _______________

13. $\dfrac{10}{11} - \dfrac{1}{11} =$ _______________

14. $\dfrac{9}{10} - \dfrac{8}{10} =$ _______________

15. $\dfrac{3}{4} - \dfrac{2}{4} =$ _______________

16. $\dfrac{4}{8} - \dfrac{2}{8} =$ _______________

17. $\dfrac{11}{12} - \dfrac{9}{12} =$ _______________

18. $\dfrac{8}{9} - \dfrac{6}{9} =$ _______________

19. $\dfrac{7}{11} - \dfrac{6}{11} =$ _______________

20. $\dfrac{9}{10} - \dfrac{6}{10} =$ _______________

21. $\dfrac{3}{4} - \dfrac{1}{4} =$ _______________

22. $\dfrac{11}{12} - \dfrac{8}{12} =$ _______________

23. $\dfrac{2}{5} - \dfrac{1}{5} =$ _______________

24. $\dfrac{4}{11} - \dfrac{3}{11} =$ _______________

25. $\dfrac{4}{7} - \dfrac{2}{7} =$ _______________

26. $\dfrac{8}{9} - \dfrac{5}{9} =$ _______________

27. $\dfrac{3}{8} - \dfrac{2}{8} =$ _______________

28. $\dfrac{8}{10} - \dfrac{5}{10} =$ _______________

29. $\dfrac{4}{5} - \dfrac{2}{5} =$ _______________

30. $\dfrac{3}{7} - \dfrac{2}{7} =$ _______________

31. $\dfrac{4}{8} - \dfrac{1}{8} =$ _______________

32. $\dfrac{6}{11} - \dfrac{4}{11} =$ _______________

33. $\dfrac{11}{12} - \dfrac{10}{12} =$ _______________

34. $\dfrac{3}{6} - \dfrac{2}{6} =$ _______________

35. $\dfrac{7}{9} - \dfrac{4}{9} =$ _______________

36. $\dfrac{4}{6} - \dfrac{2}{6} =$ _______________

37. $\dfrac{7}{8} - \dfrac{5}{8} =$ _______________

38. $\dfrac{7}{9} - \dfrac{1}{9} =$ _______________

39. $\dfrac{3}{11} - \dfrac{2}{11} =$ _______________

40. $\dfrac{6}{12} - \dfrac{5}{12} =$ _______________

41. $\dfrac{2}{10} - \dfrac{1}{10} =$ _______________

42. $\dfrac{4}{5} - \dfrac{1}{5} =$ _______________

43. $\dfrac{6}{8} - \dfrac{5}{8} =$ _______________

44. $\dfrac{2}{7} - \dfrac{1}{7} =$ _______________

45. $\dfrac{4}{6} - \dfrac{3}{6} =$ _______________

46. $\dfrac{8}{11} - \dfrac{7}{11} =$ _______________

47. $\dfrac{9}{10} - \dfrac{7}{10} =$ _______________

48. $\dfrac{8}{12} - \dfrac{4}{12} =$ _______________

49. $\dfrac{5}{6} - \dfrac{4}{6} =$ _______________

50. $\dfrac{9}{11} - \dfrac{7}{11} =$ _______________

51. $\dfrac{7}{8} - \dfrac{6}{8} =$ _______________

52. $\dfrac{8}{9} - \dfrac{2}{9} =$ _______________

53. $\dfrac{10}{11} - \dfrac{4}{11} =$ _______________

54. $\dfrac{3}{5} - \dfrac{2}{5} =$ _______________

55. $\dfrac{6}{7} - \dfrac{1}{7} =$ _______________

56. $\dfrac{3}{6} - \dfrac{1}{6} =$ _______________

57. $\dfrac{5}{12} - \dfrac{1}{12} =$ _______________

58. $\dfrac{6}{8} - \dfrac{3}{8} =$ _______________

59. $\dfrac{7}{12} - \dfrac{2}{12} =$ _______________

60. $\dfrac{6}{7} - \dfrac{3}{7} =$ _______________

Area and Perimeter: Rectangles and Triangles

1.

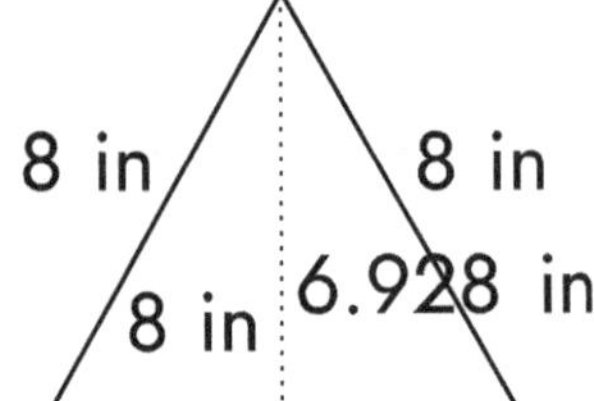

2.

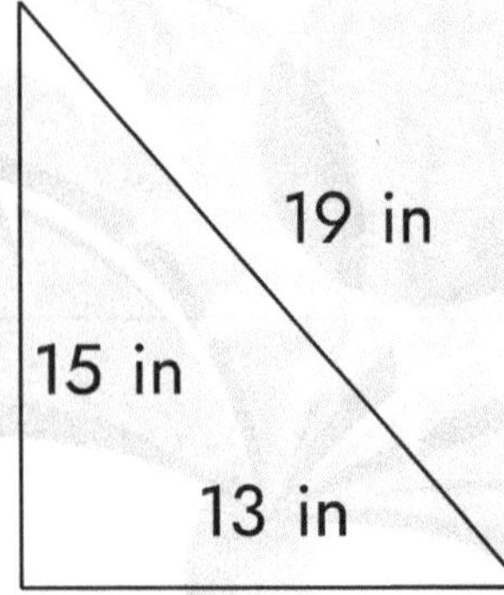

3.

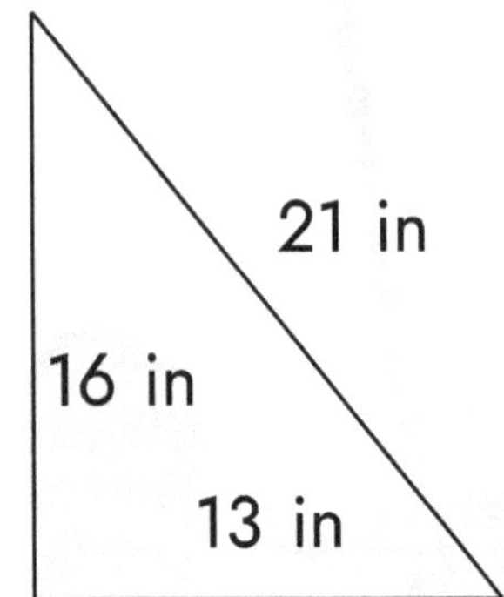

4.

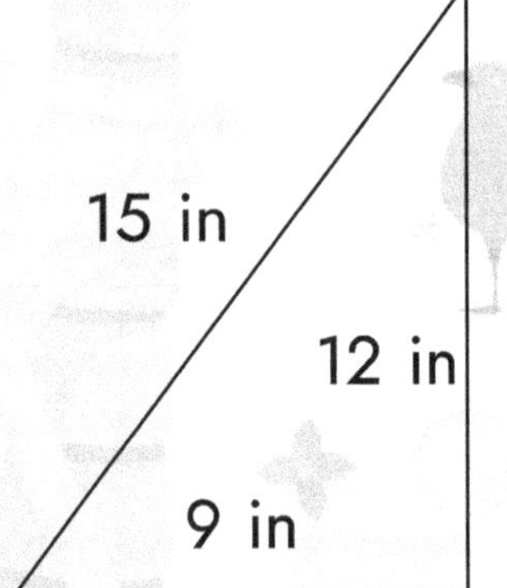

5.

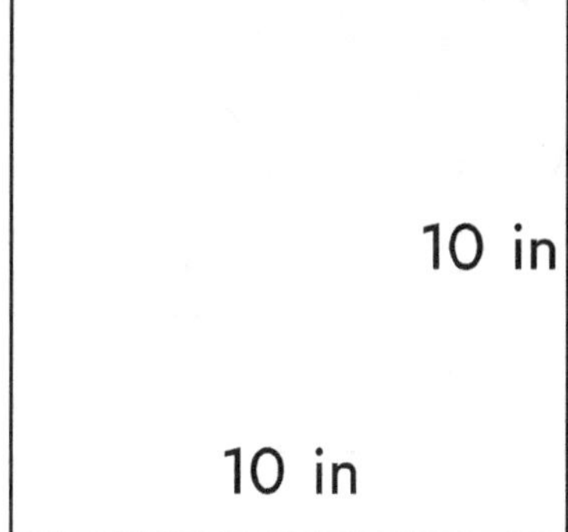

6.

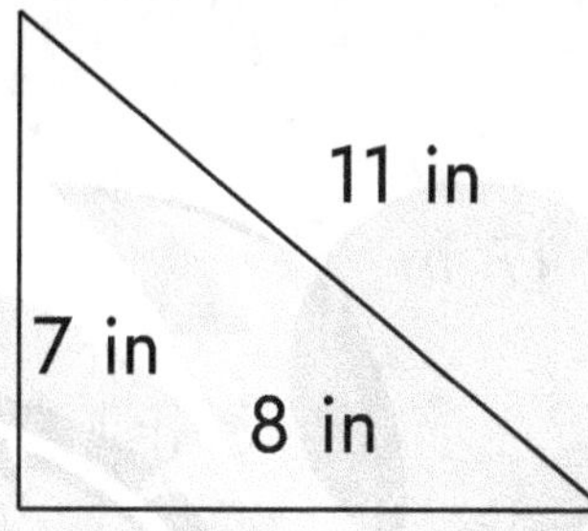

7.

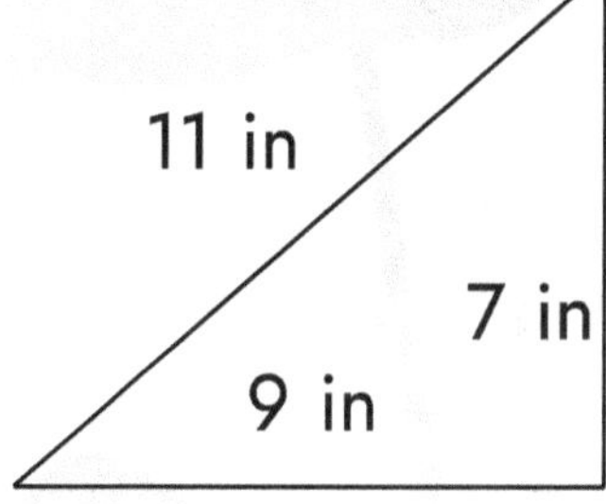

8.

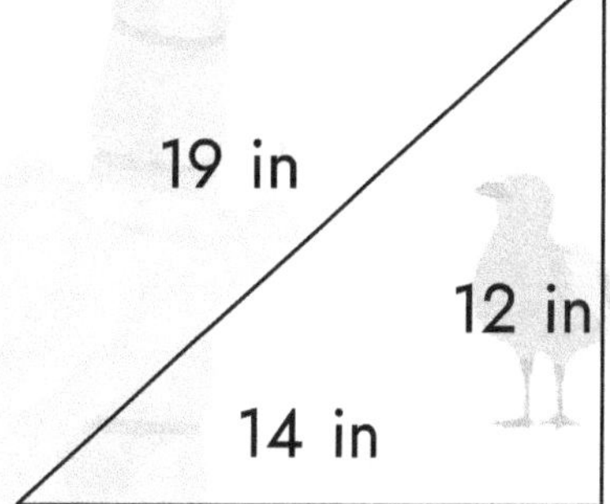

9.

17 in
13 in
11 in

10.

10 in
10 in
8.660 in
10 in

11.

11 in
8 in
7 in

12.

6 in
6 in
5.196 in
6 in

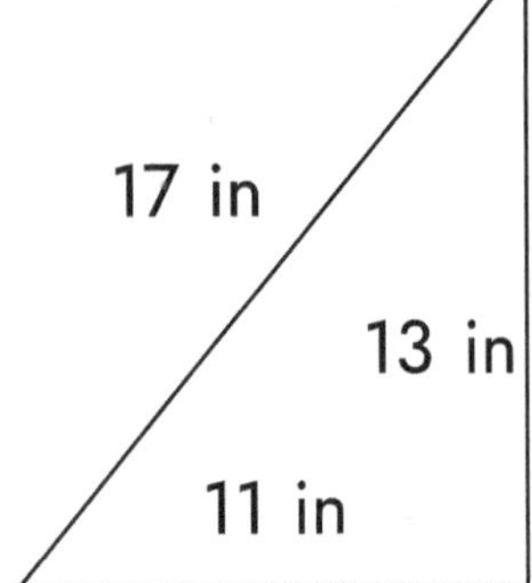

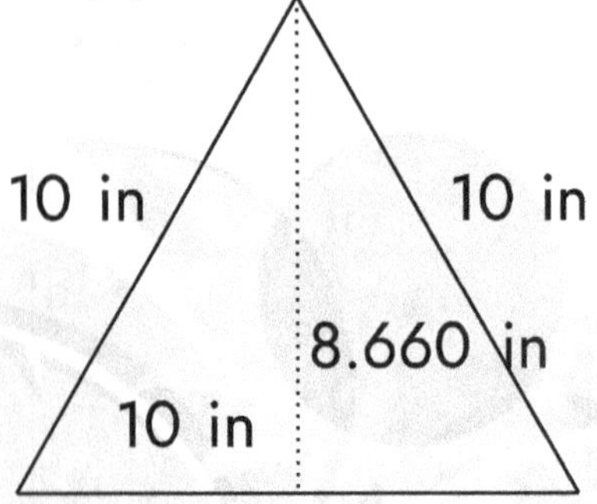

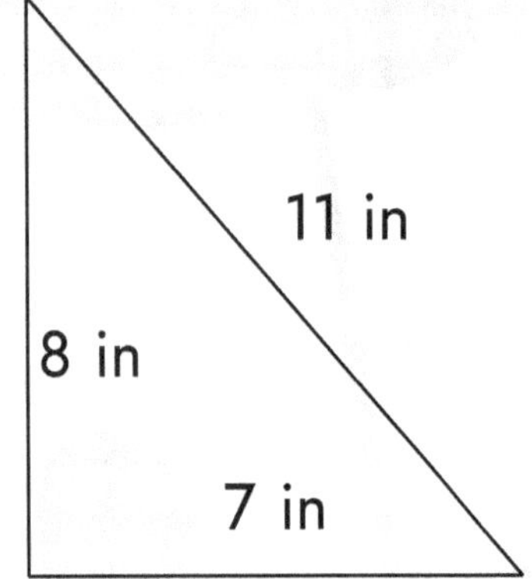

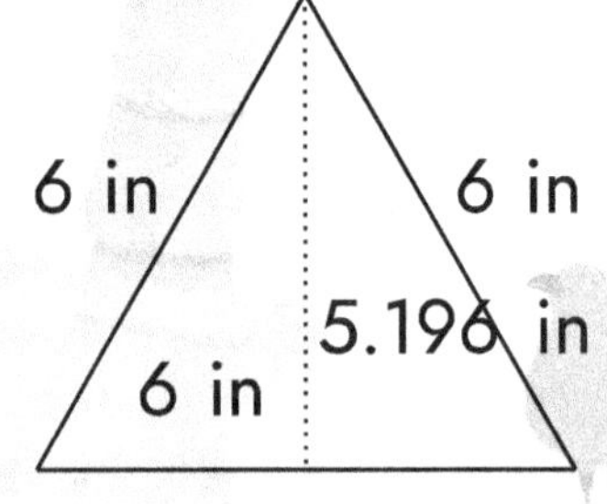

SUMMER MATH WORKBOOK
NAME:
BUILDING ACTIVITIES

13.

7 in
7 in
6.062 in
7 in

14.

7 in
8 in

15.

13 in
10 in
7 in

16.

13 in
18 in

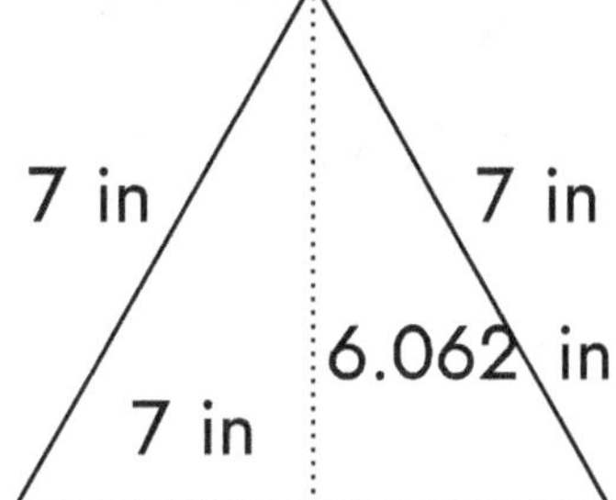

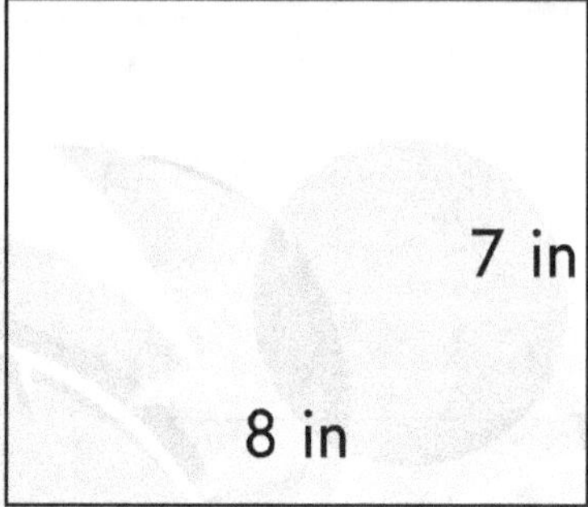

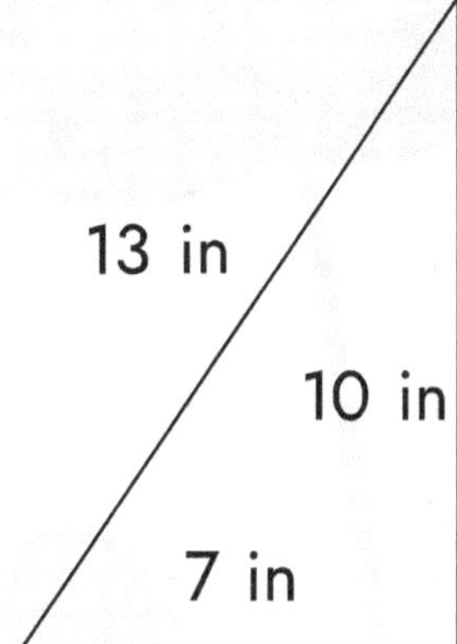

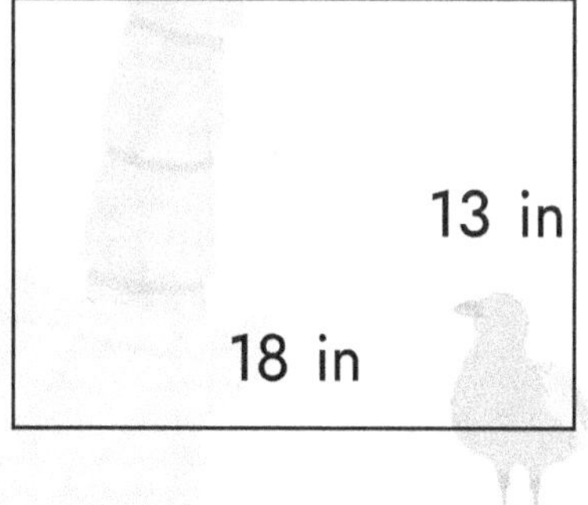

SUMMER MATH WORKBOOK
NAME:
BUILDING ACTIVITIES

17.

8 in
8 in
6.928 in
8 in

18.

13 in
10 in
8 in

19.

15 in
10 in
11 in

20.

8 in
9 in

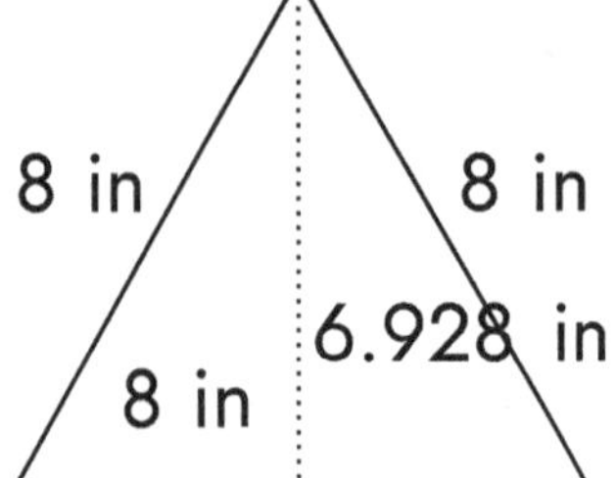

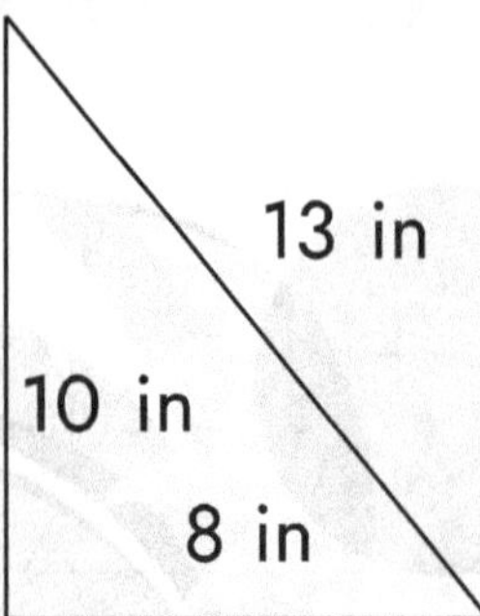

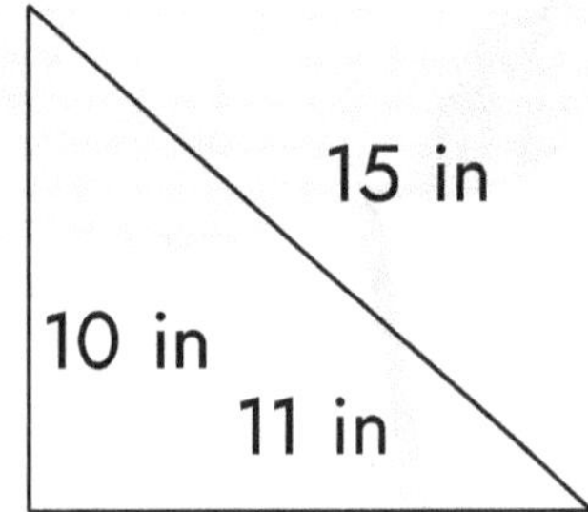

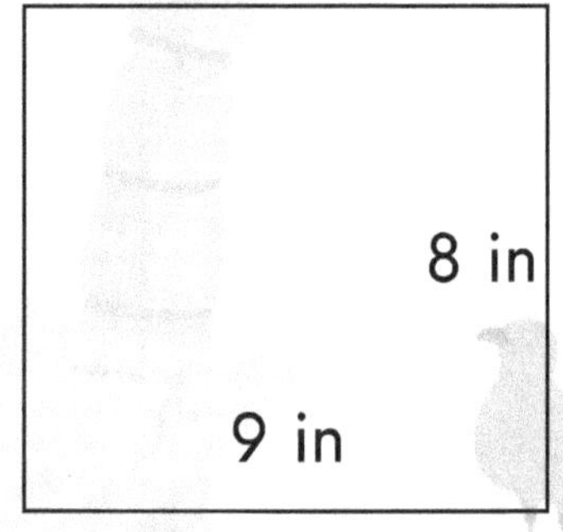

21.

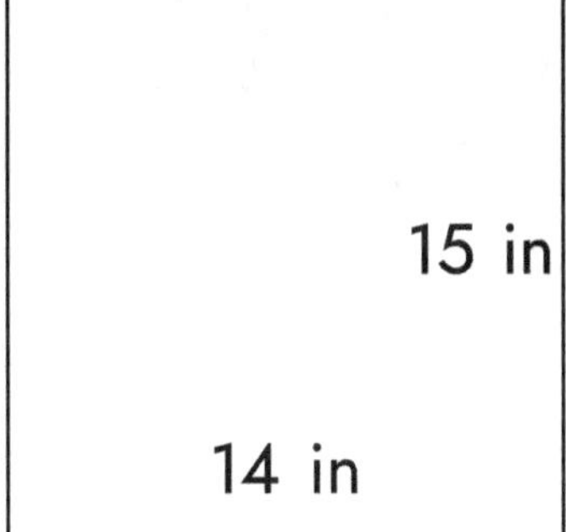

22.

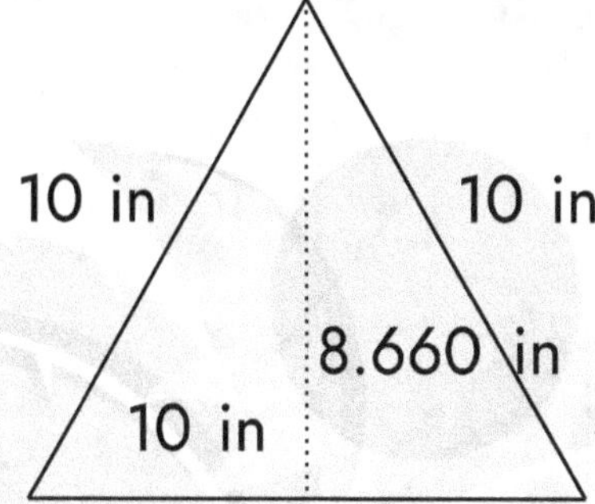

23.

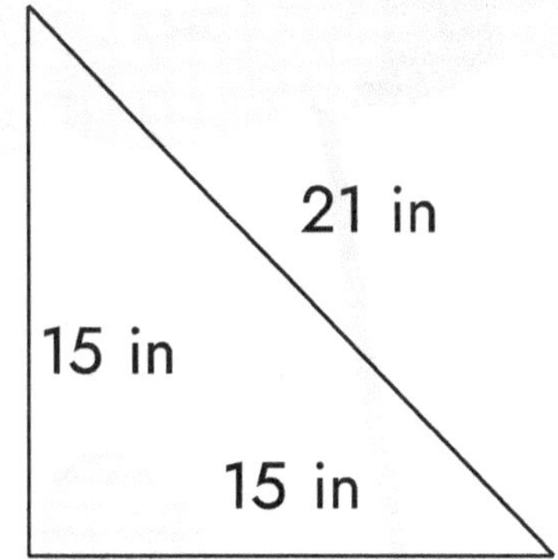

24.

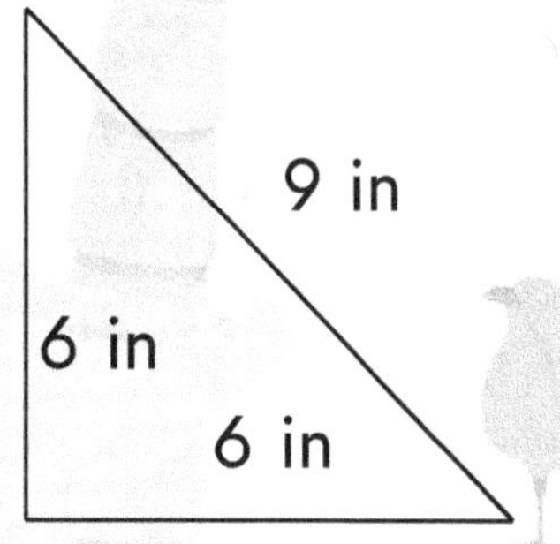

25.

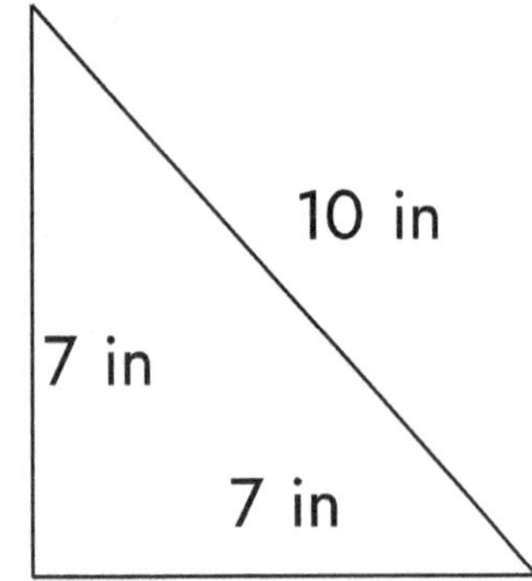

26.

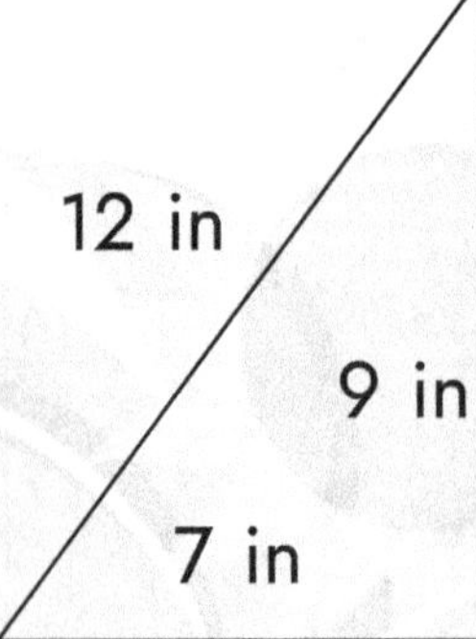

27.

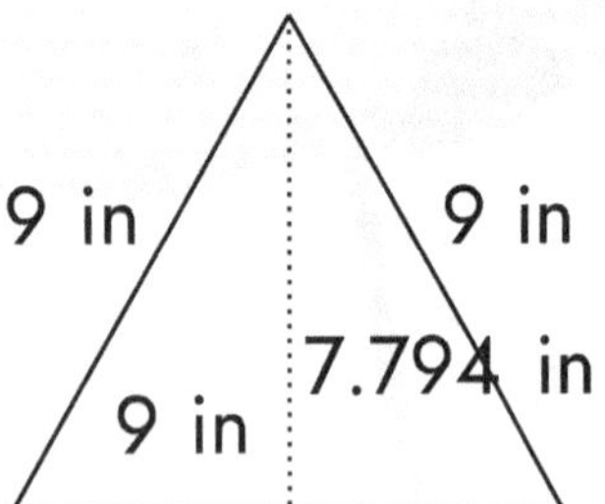

28.

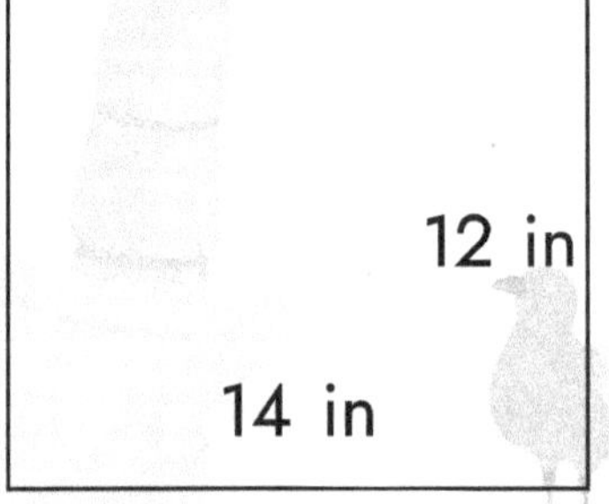

SUMMER MATH WORKBOOK
NAME:
BUILDING ACTIVITIES

29.

15 in
8 in
12 in

30.

14 in
11 in
8 in

31.

9 in
9 in
9 in
7.794 in

32.

17 in
17 in
14.722 in
17 in

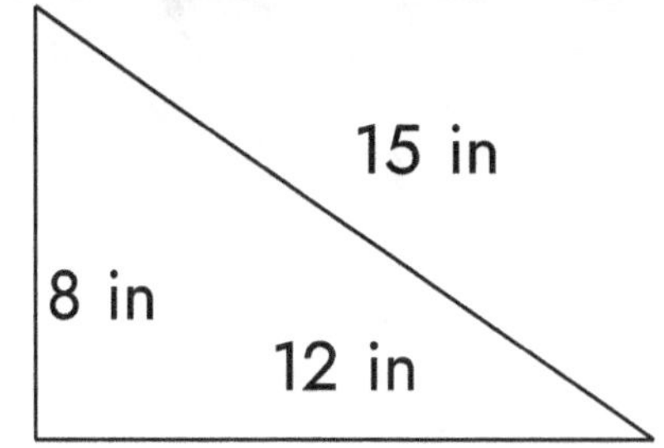

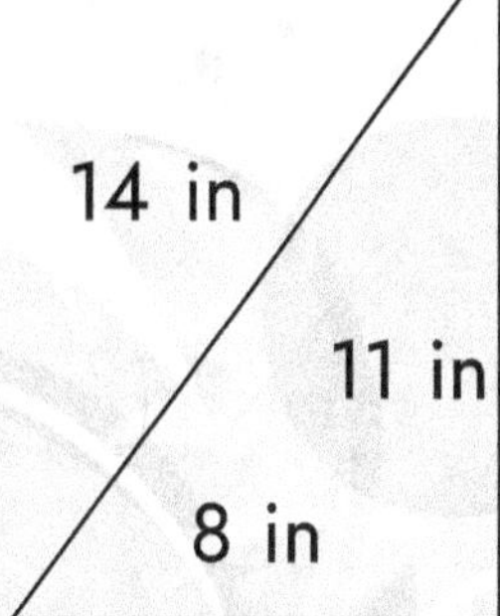

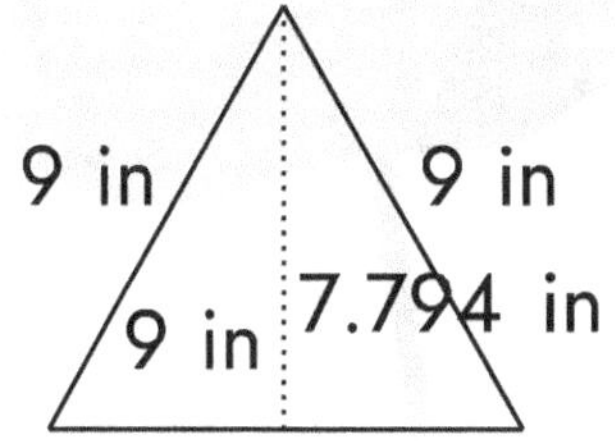

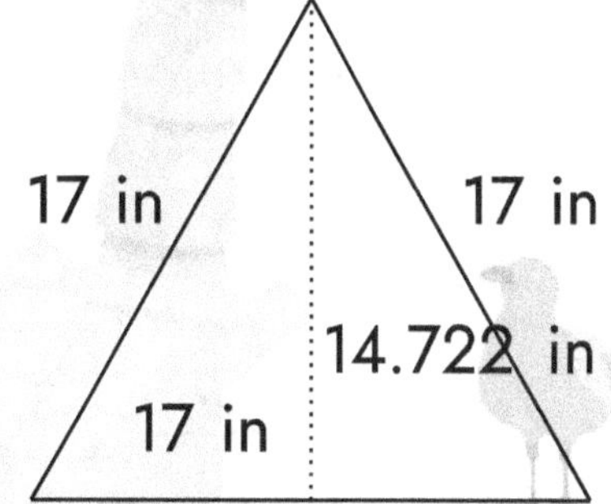

33.

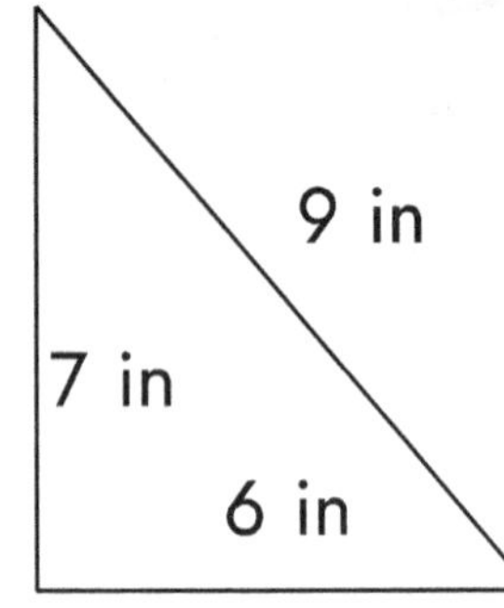

34.

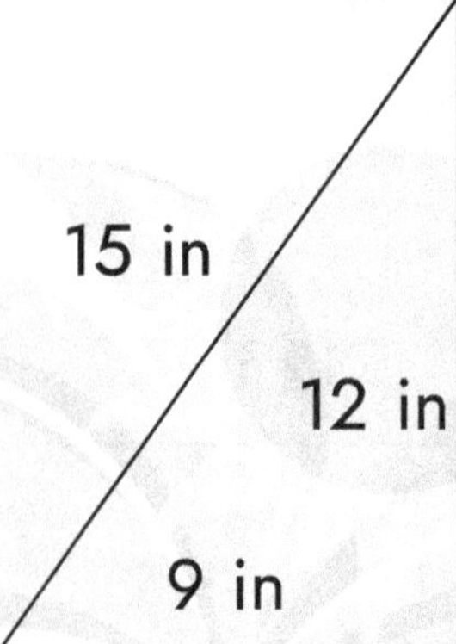

35.

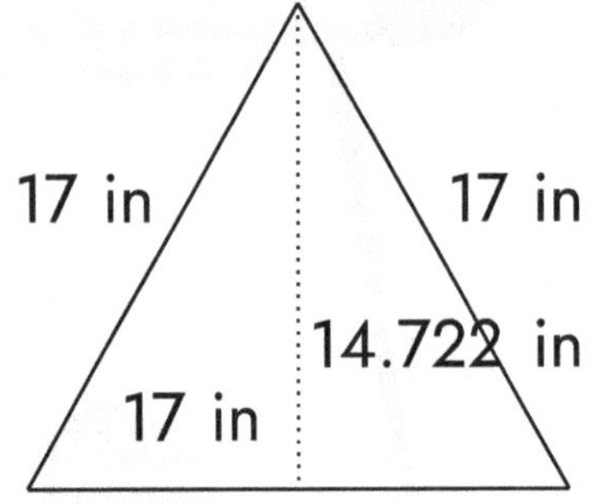

36.

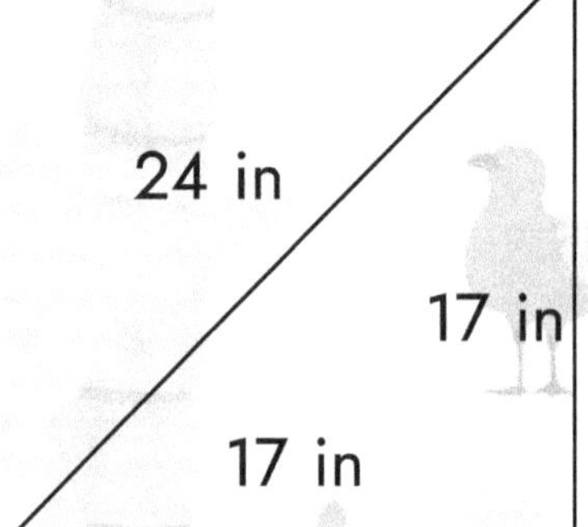

37.

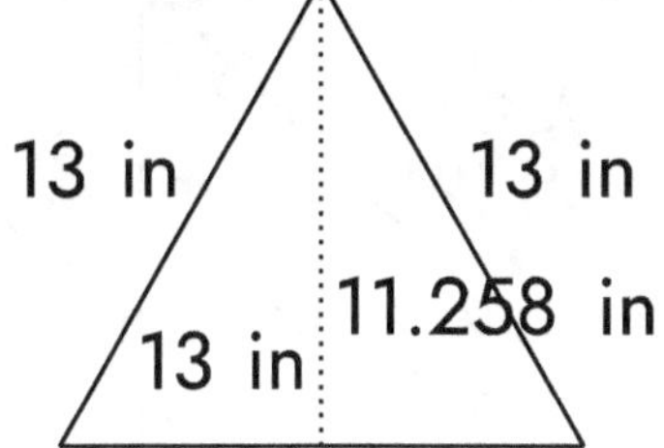

38.

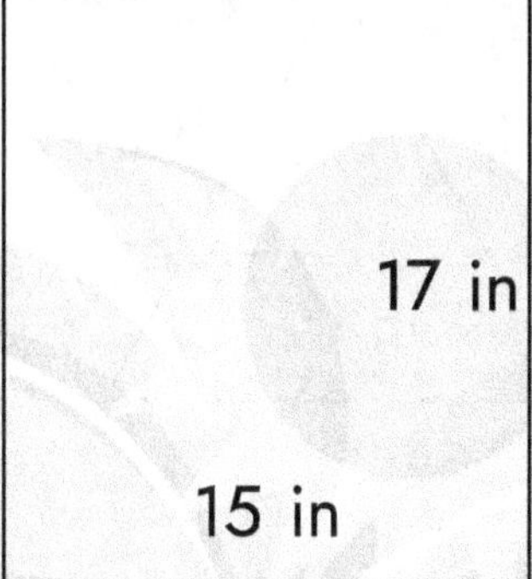

39.

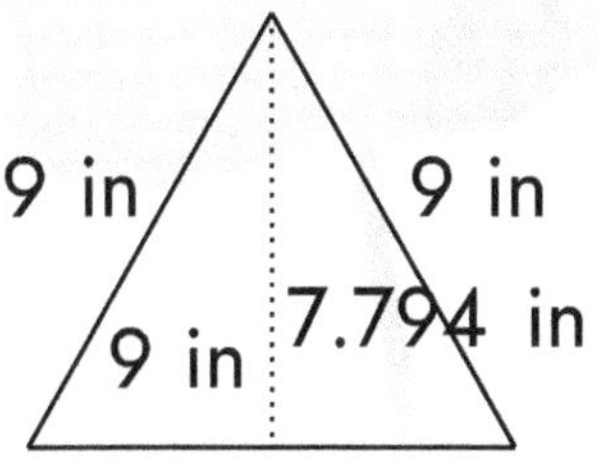

40.

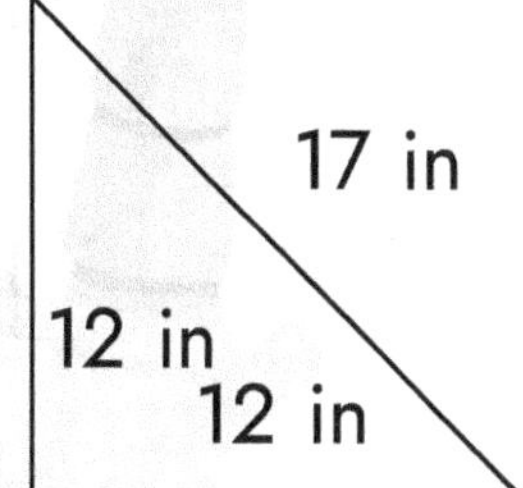

SUMMER MATH WORKBOOK
NAME:
BUILDING ACTIVITIES

41.

9 in
9 in
9 in
7.794 in

42.

13 in
9 in
9 in

43.

12 in
17 in

44.

11 in
10 in

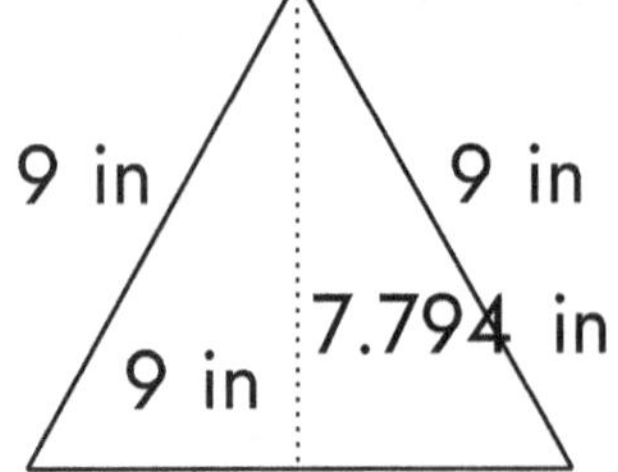

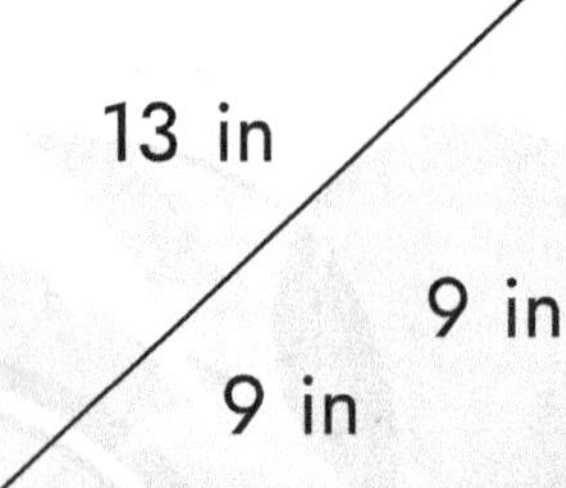

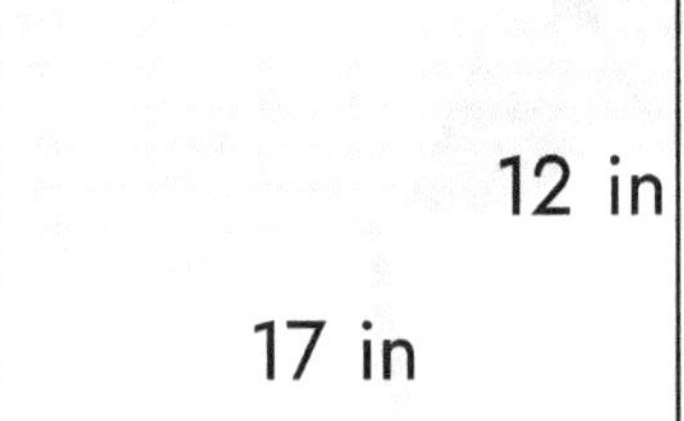

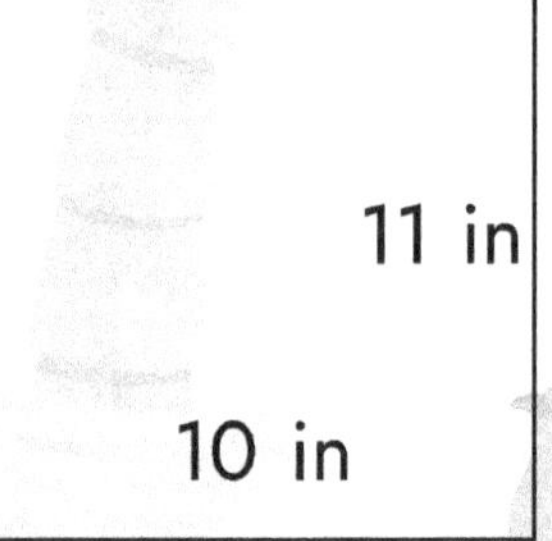

45.

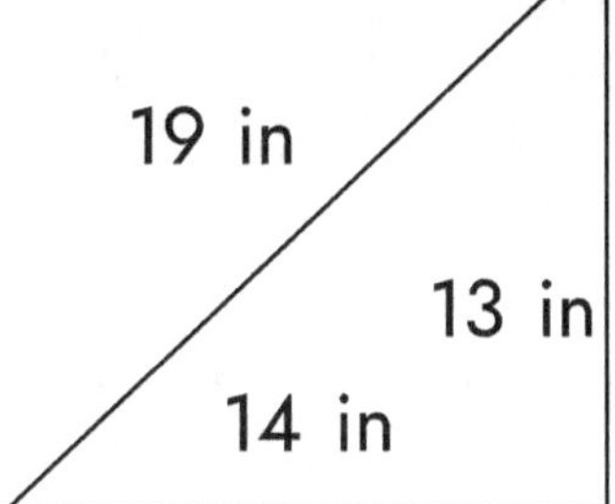

46.

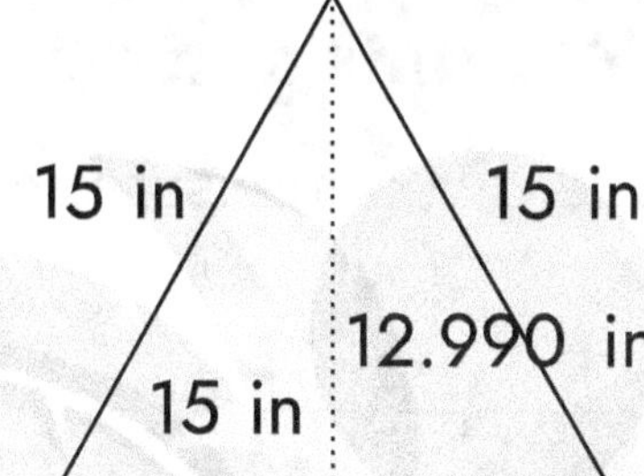

47.

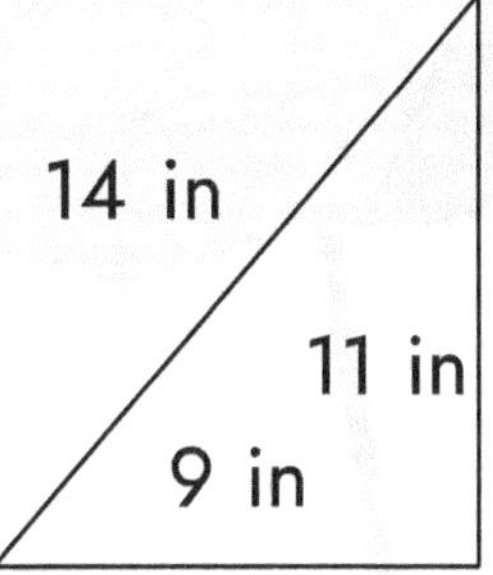

48.

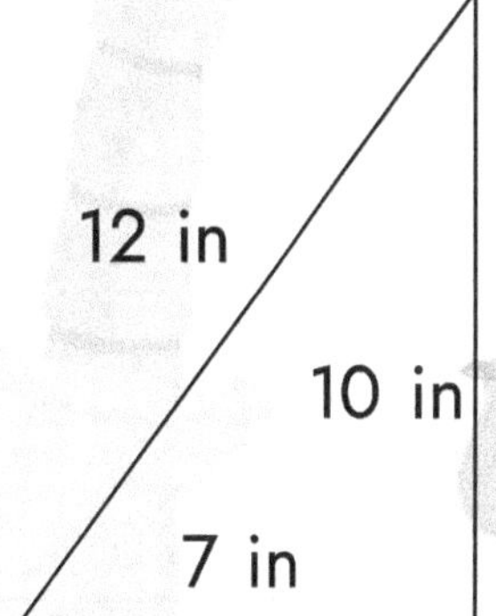

Metric Weights and Measures

Convert the given measures to new units.

1. 35 t = _______________ kg

2. 45 t = _______________ g

3. 96 km = _______________ m

4. 43 L = _______________ mL

5. 48 kL = _______________ L

6. 41 km = _______________ cm

7. 98 kg = _______________ t

8. 81 L = _______________ kL

9. 96 mL = _______________ kL

10. 89 kg = _______________ t

11. 25 km = _______________ m

12. 45 kL = _______________ L

13. 60 mL = _______________ L

14. 57 kg = _______________ t

15. 42 cm = _______________ km

16. 96 L = _______________ mL

17. 19 kg = _______________ g

18. 60 km = _______________ m

19. 47 cm = _______________ km

20. 14 mL = _______________ kL

21. 36 L = _______________ mL

22. 16 km = _______________ cm

23. 44 m = _______________ km

24. 74 L = _______________ kL

25. 50 L = _______________ mL

26. 21 mL = _______________ kL

27. 25 m = _______________ km

28. 63 t = _______________ kg

29. 89 kg = _______________ g

30. 26 kg = _______________ t

31. 78 L = _________________ kL   **32.** 72 L = _________________ kL

33. 17 kL = _________________ L   **34.** 42 km = _________________ m

35. 93 kL = _________________ mL   **36.** 92 kg = _________________ t

37. 69 t = _________________ g   **38.** 47 t = _________________ kg

39. 49 g = _________________ kg   **40.** 15 kL = _________________ mL

41. 73 g = _________________ kg   **42.** 16 kL = _________________ L

43. 70 t = _________________ kg   **44.** 88 kg = _________________ t

45. 99 t = _________________ kg   **46.** 53 L = _________________ kL

Fractions Quiz

1. What is 1/2 - 1/2?

    A. 1/2

    B. 1/2

    C. 0

    D. -3/2

2. What is 1/10 + 8/10?

    A. 9/10

    B. 4/5

    C. 4/5

    D. 11/10

3. What is 4/6 + 4/6?

    A. 2/3

    B. 11/6

    C. 4/3

    D. 1

4. What is 4/5 + 4/5?

    A. 8/5

    B. 2

    C. 7/5

    D. 4/5

5. What is 2/9 + 2/9?

    A. 1/9

    B. 7/9

    C. 4/9

    D. 2/9

6. What is 4/5 - 1/5?

    A. 3/5

    B. 1/5

    C. 4/5

    D. 4/5

7. What is 1/3 + 1/3?

    A. 2/3

    B. 1/3

    C. 1

    D. 0

8. What is 1/6 + 1/6?

    A. 1/2

    B. 0

    C. 1/2

    D. 1/3

9. What is 6/7 + 5/7?

    A. 11/7

    B. 6/7

    C. 10/7

    D. 12/7

10. What is 6/10 - 2/10?

    A. 2/5

    B. 1/2

    C. 3/10

    D. 3/10

11. What is 1/5 + 2/5?

    A. 3/5

    B. 1

    C. 0

    D. 2/5

12. What is 4/10 + 2/10?

    A. 3/5

    B. 9/10

    C. 1/10

    D. 3/10

13. What is 3/4 + 2/4?

    A. 2

    B. 5/4

    C. 1/4

    D. 1/2

14. What is 3/5 - 2/5?

    A. -1/5

    B. 2/5

    C. 4/5

    D. 1/5

15. What is 1/3 - 2/3?

    A. 1/3

    B. 1

    C. 1/3

    D. -2/3

16. What is 1/6 - 2/6?

    A. -1/6

    B. 1/6

    C. 2/3

    D. 1/6

ANSWERS

Page 1: Three-Digit Addition

1. 1,403 **2.** 766 **3.** 706 **4.** 768 **5.** 901 **6.** 945 **7.** 1,207

8. 1,405 **9.** 1,082 **10.** 1,151 **11.** 1,464 **12.** 1,148 **13.** 595 **14.** 605

15. 686 **16.** 894 **17.** 1,353 **18.** 1,312 **19.** 830 **20.** 1,045 **21.** 1,707

22. 1,003 **23.** 729 **24.** 679 **25.** 1,428 **26.** 1,609 **27.** 1,234 **28.** 1,718

29. 1,221 **30.** 626 **31.** 1,078 **32.** 621 **33.** 1,077 **34.** 633 **35.** 1,184

36. 1,361 **37.** 1,384 **38.** 701 **39.** 1,055 **40.** 1,299 **41.** 1,226 **42.** 891

43. 1,692 **44.** 806 **45.** 1,343 **46.** 876 **47.** 770 **48.** 1,241 **49.** 1,692

50. 1,080

Page 3: Three-Digit Subtraction

1. 184 **2.** 368 **3.** 25 **4.** 58 **5.** 405 **6.** 78 **7.** 45 **8.** 68

9. 341 **10.** 332 **11.** 101 **12.** 81 **13.** 372 **14.** 33 **15.** 366 **16.** 55

17. 259 **18.** 52 **19.** 392 **20.** 401 **21.** 43 **22.** 56 **23.** 32 **24.** 3

25. 243 **26.** 337 **27.** 107 **28.** 12 **29.** 269 **30.** 52 **31.** 319 **32.** 274

33. 40 **34.** 171 **35.** 689 **36.** 343 **37.** 699 **38.** 24 **39.** 153 **40.** 153

41. 71 **42.** 126 **43.** 136 **44.** 82 **45.** 12

Page 5: Mixed Two-Digit Practice

1. 1,942 **2.** 91 **3.** 220 **4.** 668 **5.** 1,207 **6.** 1,594 **7.** 64

8. 487 **9.** 120 **10.** 187 **11.** 130 **12.** 1,617 **13.** 1 **14.** 943

15. 1,103 **16.** 398 **17.** 25 **18.** 692 **19.** 1,083 **20.** 1,277 **21.** 95

22. 1,128   **23.** 459   **24.** 764   **25.** 1,051   **26.** 401   **27.** 261   **28.** 69

29. 1,070   **30.** 1,023   **31.** 432   **32.** 26   **33.** 46   **34.** 336   **35.** 983

36. 1,139   **37.** 1,011   **38.** 579   **39.** 1,763   **40.** 429   **41.** 313   **42.** 550

43. 867   **44.** 1,285   **45.** 1,708   **46.** 421   **47.** 118   **48.** 160   **49.** 31

50. 1,539   **51.** 674   **52.** 150   **53.** 1,698   **54.** 1,452   **55.** 705   **56.** 1,408

Page 8:   Addition with Regrouping

1. 16,210   **2.** 17,110   **3.** 11,120   **4.** 19,325   **5.** 16,123   **6.** 12,251

7. 14,415   **8.** 17,133   **9.** 12,228   **10.** 11,131   **11.** 11,223   **12.** 11,420

13. 13,570   **14.** 13,113   **15.** 11,352   **16.** 11,213   **17.** 11,241   **18.** 13,225

19. 11,270   **20.** 12,740   **21.** 15,714   **22.** 17,210   **23.** 16,615   **24.** 12,123

25. 13,654   **26.** 17,120   **27.** 11,343   **28.** 16,131   **29.** 14,311   **30.** 15,175

31. 11,213   **32.** 12,232   **33.** 17,112   **34.** 11,180   **35.** 18,140   **36.** 17,110

37. 16,313   **38.** 11,312   **39.** 12,111   **40.** 12,512   **41.** 16,561   **42.** 11,450

43. 16,111   **44.** 13,134   **45.** 14,340   **46.** 11,323   **47.** 17,810   **48.** 12,222

49. 14,115   **50.** 11,110   **51.** 12,230   **52.** 12,612   **53.** 11,731   **54.** 15,222

55. 11,110   **56.** 14,650

Page 11:   Subtraction with Regrouping

1. 3,669   **2.** 2,737   **3.** 467   **4.** 559   **5.** 539   **6.** 4,509

7. 3,859   **8.** 837   **9.** 2,885   **10.** 849   **11.** 3,859   **12.** 829

13. 827   **14.** 2,326   **15.** 4,245   **16.** 1,828   **17.** 776   **18.** 609

19. 1,389   **20.** 463   **21.** 1,747   **22.** 649   **23.** 2,864   **24.** 524

25. 678   **26.** 5,837   **27.** 1,828   **28.** 848   **29.** 529   **30.** 1,308

31. 1,309   **32.** 808   **33.** 1,718   **34.** 687   **35.** 5,019   **36.** 4,548

37. 828   **38.** 889   **39.** 588   **40.** 827   **41.** 849   **42.** 1,829

43. 749   **44.** 4,669   **45.** 3,848   **46.** 2,804   **47.** 759   **48.** 1,889

49. 4,807   **50.** 4,535   **51.** 4,758   **52.** 865   **53.** 1,178   **54.** 5,825

55. 3,325   **56.** 768

Page 14:   Three-Addends

1. 1,587   **2.** 1,089   **3.** 1,175   **4.** 1,566   **5.** 1,828   **6.** 2,536   **7.** 1,390

8. 1,443   **9.** 1,627   **10.** 1,917   **11.** 1,536   **12.** 1,690   **13.** 1,187   **14.** 1,000

15. 2,104   **16.** 1,037   **17.** 954   **18.** 2,204   **19.** 1,014   **20.** 2,263   **21.** 1,869

22. 1,828   **23.** 2,063   **24.** 1,876   **25.** 1,803   **26.** 1,463   **27.** 1,060   **28.** 1,042

29. 1,590   **30.** 1,725   **31.** 1,316   **32.** 1,388   **33.** 1,539   **34.** 2,323   **35.** 1,456

36. 1,106   **37.** 2,013   **38.** 1,120   **39.** 2,177   **40.** 1,789   **41.** 1,668   **42.** 1,055

43. 1,671   **44.** 2,175

Page 17:   Place Value

1. 6 ten thousands   **2.** 5 thousands   **3.** 9 ones

4. 1 hundred   **5.** 2 ten thousands   **6.** 5 thousands

7. 2 ten thousands   **8.** 6 thousands   **9.** 8 thousands

10. 8 tens   **11.** 9 ten thousands   **12.** 2 hundreds

13. 1 thousand   **14.** 8 ones   **15.** 1 thousand

16. 5 ones   **17.** 9 thousands   **18.** 4 thousands

19. 6 hundreds   **20.** 9 tens   **21.** 2 tens

22. 3 ones   **23.** 6 hundreds   **24.** 9 hundreds

25. 4 tens   **26.** 9 tens   **27.** 2 hundreds

28. 6 ten thousands   **29.** 3 thousands   **30.** 8 tens

31. 9 ones   **32.** 9 tens

Page 19: Place Value: Expanded Notation

1. 86,629   **2.** 59,119   **3.** 92,777   **4.** 86,599   **5.** 35,005   **6.** 66,612

7. 20,809   **8.** 66,743   **9.** 25,840   **10.** 93,766   **11.** 52,809   **12.** 11,489

13. 36,105   **14.** 68,768   **15.** 57,864   **16.** 26,032   **17.** 33,900   **18.** 11,900

19. 80,875   **20.** 94,968   **21.** 73,084   **22.** 44,092   **23.** 45,393   **24.** 24,151

25. 78,165   **26.** 77,975   **27.** 92,898   **28.** 71,863   **29.** 32,304   **30.** 96,680

31. 99,218   **32.** 97,493   **33.** 90,622   **34.** 33,039   **35.** 40,578   **36.** 78,650

37. 50,486   **38.** 19,437   **39.** 21,300   **40.** 72,498   **41.** 38,578   **42.** 22,883

43. 35,764

Page 24: Multiplication: 2 x 1

1. 80   **2.** 39   **3.** 22   **4.** 48   **5.** 46   **6.** 18   **7.** 80   **8.** 66   **9.** 85

10. 50   **11.** 62   **12.** 26   **13.** 24   **14.** 40   **15.** 44   **16.** 93   **17.** 69   **18.** 33

19. 88   **20.** 84   **21.** 36   **22.** 60   **23.** 68   **24.** 42   **25.** 90   **26.** 96   **27.** 20

28. 63   **29.** 28   **30.** 51   **31.** 64   **32.** 55   **33.** 66   **34.** 62   **35.** 55   **36.** 44

Page 26: Multiplication: 3 x 1

1. 333   **2.** 960   **3.** 484   **4.** 550   **5.** 690   **6.** 505   **7.** 393   **8.** 400

9. 804   **10.** 608   **11.** 396   **12.** 844   **13.** 906   **14.** 880   **15.** 933   **16.** 488

17. 888   **18.** 402   **19.** 828   **20.** 669   **21.** 600   **22.** 444   **23.** 353   **24.** 482

25. 990   **26.** 693   **27.** 696   **28.** 866   **29.** 404   **30.** 422   **31.** 426   **32.** 804

33. 939   **34.** 664   **35.** 369   **36.** 900

Page 28: Multiplication: 4 x 1

1. 2,422   **2.** 2,644   **3.** 6,636   **4.** 9,300   **5.** 9,696   **6.** 8,800

7. 6,009   **8.** 9,660   **9.** 8,822   **10.** 6,008   **11.** 2,424   **12.** 5,050

13. 6,244   **14.** 2,808   **15.** 5,373   **16.** 3,699   **17.** 6,063   **18.** 6,248

19. 5,055   **20.** 4,400   **21.** 4,888   **22.** 4,402   **23.** 9,966   **24.** 4,444

25. 4,406   **26.** 4,408   **27.** 8,646   **28.** 4,404   **29.** 9,666   **30.** 8,226

31. 4,088   **32.** 4,866   **33.** 6,846   **34.** 8,000   **35.** 6,669   **36.** 2,448

Page 30: Multiplication (double Digit)

1. 1,972   **2.** 564   **3.** 3,080   **4.** 3,240   **5.** 2,352   **6.** 672   **7.** 5,580

8. 1,326   **9.** 5,856   **10.** 3,915   **11.** 2,592   **12.** 2,765   **13.** 5,185   **14.** 2,320

15. 4,810   **16.** 1,456   **17.** 3,430   **18.** 6,225   **19.** 4,745   **20.** 871   **21.** 6,885

22. 286   **23.** 1,000   **24.** 1,825   **25.** 540   **26.** 2,852   **27.** 7,560   **28.** 180

29. 1,056   **30.** 4,930   **31.** 4,717   **32.** 5,244   **33.** 2,500   **34.** 7,189   **35.** 924

36. 1,734   **37.** 7,812   **38.** 5,841   **39.** 667   **40.** 1,984   **41.** 1,430   **42.** 1,083

43. 897   **44.** 720   **45.** 7,626   **46.** 2,236   **47.** 1,653   **48.** 966

Page 34: Basic Division

1. 4   **2.** 7   **3.** 8   **4.** 2   **5.** 4   **6.** 1   **7.** 1   **8.** 2   **9.** 6   **10.** 3

11. 2   **12.** 8   **13.** 4   **14.** 10   **15.** 2   **16.** 8   **17.** 3   **18.** 9   **19.** 9   **20.** 4

21. 1   **22.** 7   **23.** 2   **24.** 9   **25.** 4   **26.** 3   **27.** 9   **28.** 1   **29.** 9   **30.** 3

31. 5   **32.** 7   **33.** 7   **34.** 9   **35.** 2   **36.** 10   **37.** 4   **38.** 3   **39.** 8   **40.** 6

41. 5   **42.** 6   **43.** 9   **44.** 2   **45.** 1   **46.** 7   **47.** 8   **48.** 6   **49.** 4   **50.** 5

51. 4   **52.** 7   **53.** 7   **54.** 6   **55.** 1   **56.** 3

Page 37: Long Division (within 100)

1. 37   **2.** 62   **3.** 88   **4.** 50   **5.** 54   **6.** 32   **7.** 42   **8.** 70   **9.** 93

10. 2   **11.** 31   **12.** 85   **13.** 62   **14.** 73   **15.** 73   **16.** 17   **17.** 33   **18.** 4

19. 87   **20.** 94   **21.** 48   **22.** 65   **23.** 92   **24.** 24   **25.** 52   **26.** 97   **27.** 6

28. 69   **29.** 72   **30.** 24   **31.** 39   **32.** 1   **33.** 28   **34.** 15   **35.** 30   **36.** 99

37. 2   **38.** 7   **39.** 50   **40.** 95   **41.** 57   **42.** 59   **43.** 28   **44.** 91

Page 40: Adding Decimals

1. 1,437.97   **2.** 1,401.08   **3.** 552.65   **4.** 984.33   **5.** 1,065.94

6. 531.49   **7.** 1,563.57   **8.** 615.37   **9.** 527.62   **10.** 728.45

11. 1,160.00   **12.** 1,091.28   **13.** 1,054.06   **14.** 1,299.10   **15.** 1,063.34

16. 711.65   **17.** 757.52   **18.** 861.01   **19.** 1,467.67   **20.** 1,126.47

21. 891.37   **22.** 1,565.23   **23.** 829.17   **24.** 1,057.62   **25.** 507.53

26. 796.35   **27.** 909.60   **28.** 1,510.31   **29.** 717.74   **30.** 830.23

31. 1,025.16   **32.** 1,212.07   **33.** 806.91   **34.** 1,056.58   **35.** 633.76

36. 968.12

Page 43: Subtracting Decimals

1. 853.39   **2.** 48.00   **3.** 211.41   **4.** 400.97   **5.** 2.11   **6.** 390.09

7. 264.32   **8.** 13.47   **9.** 113.72   **10.** 526.37   **11.** 73.13   **12.** 434.19

13. 31.39   **14.** 484.81   **15.** 55.06   **16.** 515.91   **17.** 738.88   **18.** 346.92

19. 124.00   **20.** 80.02   **21.** 79.60   **22.** 186.89   **23.** 273.00   **24.** 629.23

25. 828.26   **26.** 34.22   **27.** 156.23   **28.** 790.17   **29.** 166.58   **30.** 379.88

31. 258.00   **32.** 702.01   **33.** 491.31   **34.** 120.59   **35.** 201.23   **36.** 267.74

Page 46: Fraction Identification

1. 11/12   **2.** 3/4   **3.** 1/9   **4.** 2/3   **5.** 1/2   **6.** 1/3   **7.** 7/8

8. 4/5   **9.** 3/5   **10.** 5/7   **11.** 2/5   **12.** 1/2   **13.** 3/10   **14.** 1/4

15. 4/7   **16.** 2/3   **17.** 3/4   **18.** 2/3   **19.** 4/5   **20.** 5/6   **21.** 5/6

22. 1/2   **23.** 8/9   **24.** 1/3   **25.** 1/4   **26.** 1/10   **27.** 7/9   **28.** 2/7

29. 2/9   **30.** 1/8   **31.** 2/3   **32.** 4/9   **33.** 1/6   **34.** 3/4   **35.** 5/8

36. 3/7   **37.** 1/2   **38.** 1/2   **39.** 5/12

Page 51: Compare the Fractions

1. <   **2.** >   **3.** >   **4.** <   **5.** <   **6.** <   **7.** >   **8.** <   **9.** <   **10.** <   **11.** >

12. <   **13.** =   **14.** <   **15.** >   **16.** >   **17.** <   **18.** >   **19.** >   **20.** <   **21.** <   **22.** >

23. <   **24.** >   **25.** >   **26.** <   **27.** >   **28.** >   **29.** >   **30.** >   **31.** >   **32.** >   **33.** >

34. <   **35.** >   **36.** <   **37.** >   **38.** >   **39.** >   **40.** >

Page 54: Convert Fractions to Decimals

1. 0.98   **2.** 0.62   **3.** 0.4   **4.** 0.58   **5.** 0.46   **6.** 0.26   **7.** 0.16

8. 0.29   **9.** 0.91   **10.** 0.12   **11.** 0.5   **12.** 0.47   **13.** 0.2   **14.** 0.75

15. 0.33   **16.** 0.7   **17.** 0.56   **18.** 0.81   **19.** 0.76   **20.** 0.71   **21.** 0.72

22. 0.17   **23.** 0.17   **24.** 0.9   **25.** 0.33   **26.** 0.17   **27.** 0.47   **28.** 0.71

29. 0.5   **30.** 0.82   **31.** 0.88   **32.** 0.25   **33.** 0.16   **34.** 0.41

Page 57: Fractions Addition (Common Denominator)

1. 1/2   **2.** 3/5   **3.** 3/4   **4.** 3/4   **5.** 1/1   **6.** 5/9   **7.** 3/5

8. 2/3   **9.** 5/6   **10.** 3/5   **11.** 3/8   **12.** 6/7   **13.** 2/11   **14.** 3/4

15. 3/5   **16.** 7/9   **17.** 10/11   **18.** 3/4   **19.** 1/2   **20.** 4/5   **21.** 5/7

22. 2/3   **23.** 11/12   **24.** 7/8   **25.** 4/5   **26.** 10/11   **27.** 2/3   **28.** 1/2

29. 2/3   **30.** 6/7   **31.** 6/11   **32.** 3/4   **33.** 4/5   **34.** 7/12   **35.** 4/5

36. 1/2   **37.** 5/9   **38.** 1/2   **39.** 3/4   **40.** 6/11   **41.** 11/12   **42.** 5/11

43. 4/7   **44.** 2/3   **45.** 7/10   **46.** 1/3   **47.** 2/5   **48.** 6/7   **49.** 5/12

50. 4/11   **51.** 5/8   **52.** 5/9   **53.** 9/11   **54.** 7/8   **55.** 7/9   **56.** 1/3

57. 9/10   **58.** 5/6   **59.** 8/9   **60.** 3/10

Page 62:   Fractions Subtraction: (Common Denominator)

1. 2/7   **2.** 1/3   **3.** 2/5   **4.** 2/3   **5.** 1/9   **6.** 1/10   **7.** 1/5

8. 1/6   **9.** 1/12   **10.** 1/7   **11.** 5/8   **12.** 1/9   **13.** 9/11   **14.** 1/10

15. 1/4   **16.** 1/4   **17.** 1/6   **18.** 2/9   **19.** 1/11   **20.** 3/10   **21.** 1/2

22. 1/4   **23.** 1/5   **24.** 1/11   **25.** 2/7   **26.** 1/3   **27.** 1/8   **28.** 3/10

29. 2/5   **30.** 1/7   **31.** 3/8   **32.** 2/11   **33.** 1/12   **34.** 1/6   **35.** 1/3

36. 1/3   **37.** 1/4   **38.** 2/3   **39.** 1/11   **40.** 1/12   **41.** 1/10   **42.** 3/5

43. 1/8   **44.** 1/7   **45.** 1/6   **46.** 1/11   **47.** 1/5   **48.** 1/3   **49.** 1/6

50. 2/11   **51.** 1/8   **52.** 2/3   **53.** 6/11   **54.** 1/5   **55.** 5/7   **56.** 1/3

57. 1/3   **58.** 3/8   **59.** 5/12   **60.** 3/7

Page 67:   Area and Perimeter: Rectangles and Triangles

1. P=24 A=27.71   **2.** P=47 A=97.5   **3.** P=50 A=104

4. P=36 A=54   **5.** P=40 A=100   **6.** P=26 A=28

7. P=27 A=31.5   **8.** P=45 A=84   **9.** P=41 A=71.5

10. P=30 A=43.3   **11.** P=26 A=28   **12.** P=18 A=15.59

13. P=21 A=21.22

14. P=30 A=56

15. P=30 A=35

16. P=62 A=234

17. P=24 A=27.71

18. P=31 A=40

19. P=36 A=55

20. P=34 A=72

21. P=58 A=210

22. P=30 A=43.3

23. P=51 A=112.5

24. P=21 A=18

25. P=24 A=24.5

26. P=28 A=31.5

27. P=27 A=35.07

28. P=52 A=168

29. P=35 A=48

30. P=33 A=44

31. P=27 A=35.07

32. P=51 A=125.14

33. P=22 A=21

34. P=36 A=54

35. P=51 A=125.14

36. P=58 A=144.5

37. P=39 A=73.18

38. P=64 A=255

39. P=27 A=35.07

40. P=41 A=72

41. P=27 A=35.07

42. P=31 A=40.5

43. P=58 A=204

44. P=42 A=110

45. P=46 A=91

46. P=45 A=97.42

47. P=34 A=49.5

48. P=29 A=35

Page 79: Metric Weights and Measures

1. 35,000

2. 45,000,000

3. 96,000

4. 43,000

5. 48,000

6. 4,100,000

7. 0.098

8. 0.081

9. 0.000096

10. 0.089

11. 25,000

12. 45,000

13. 0.060

14. 0.057

15. 0.00042

16. 96,000

17. 19,000

18. 60,000

19. 0.00047

20. 0.000014

21. 36,000

22. 1,600,000

23. 0.044

24. 0.074

25. 50,000

26. 0.000021

27. 0.025

28. 63,000

29. 89,000

30. 0.026

31. 0.078

32. 0.072

33. 17,000

34. 42,000

35. 93,000,000

36. 0.092

37. 69,000,000   **38.** 47,000   **39.** 0.049   **40.** 15,000,000

41. 0.073   **42.** 16,000   **43.** 70,000   **44.** 0.088

45. 99,000   **46.** 0.053

Page 82: Fractions Quiz

1. 0	**5.** 4/9	**9.** 11/7	**13.** 5/4
2. 9/10	**6.** 3/5	**10.** 2/5	**14.** 1/5
3. 4/3	**7.** 2/3	**11.** 3/5	**15.** 1/3
4. 8/5	**8.** 1/3	**12.** 3/5	**16.** 1/6